THOMAS
JEFFERSON,

His Many Talents

Th Jefferson

THOMAS JEFFERSON,
His Many Talents

JOHANNA JOHNSTON

Illustrated by Richard Bergere

DODD, MEAD & COMPANY - NEW YORK

ACKNOWLEDGMENT

The author wishes to express her gratitude to Dr. Bernard Mayo, Professor of American History at the University of Virginia, author of JEFFERSON HIMSELF: THE PERSONAL NARRATIVE OF A MANY-SIDED AMERICAN and other works on Jefferson, for checking the manuscript of this book for accuracy and correcting it in matters of detail.

To W. W. W.

AUTHOR'S NOTE

FROM THE VERY FIRST WHEEL TO THE OUTER-SPACE ROCKET, from cave-homes to skyscrapers, the people who have changed the world and helped mankind to a better life have had one thing in common—inquiring minds.

Archimedes stepped into his bath and saw the water rise, Copernicus watched the stars and planets moving across the sky, Galileo saw a lantern swinging back and forth on a long chain. Each of them really looked and *saw* these everyday things and, instead of dismissing them as nothing remarkable, each asked "Why?" And so each of them moved mankind another giant step toward understanding and coping with the surrounding world.

Thomas Jefferson had this kind of mind to a unique degree. Nothing was so ordinary or taken-for-granted that it could escape his scrutiny and his questioning. And because he was extraordinarily talented in dozens of different ways— one of the most versatile geniuses who ever lived—this tireless interest in everything led him to accomplish surprising things.

Book after book after book has been written about his achievements as a political philosopher and statesman, and

7

about the way he helped move the world to a new concept of democracy.

This book does not tell that story again, except as a background to all the *other* things he did, from evolving a formula for waterproof mortar, to classifying fossils, to pioneering in the study of North American geography. The variety of these other things is staggering, and in their very range, from humble to dramatic, they show a truly inquiring mind in action.

They show, in fact, a man who could not help looking at the way men governed themselves and thinking of a better system, because this was how he looked at everything in life—with eyes that saw and a mind that asked "Why?" and "How can it be better?"

It is a way of looking at things we all can strive for and, as heirs of the better world he helped make for us, do our part toward making it still better in the future.

—JOHANNA JOHNSTON

New York City
May, 1961

8

CONTENTS

"A mind always employed is always happy."

THOMAS JEFFERSON

ARCHITECT AND BUILDER

I.

HE HAD A WAY OF LOOKING AT EVERYTHING AS THOUGH IT were brand-new. And a way of asking questions about everything, too—of himself, and anyone who was around.

A plow, for instance.

What is a plow?

He stared at the plowshare, driving deep into the hard, red earth of his father's lands in the hill country of western Virginia. He saw it breaking the earth and lifting it so that it fell again, crumbled and loosened.

A plow, he realized, is a simple and wonderful tool, the purpose of which is to break the hard crust of the earth and make it ready for the planting of seeds. He looked at the plow and saw how it had been designed to achieve this purpose—the slanted V of the plowshare held and balanced and thrust forward by the beam, so that pushed or pulled across a field, it could not fail to dig and lift the earth as it went.

It seemed very beautiful to him in its simple efficiency, a real magic wand for turning the wilderness into a fertile garden—the most useful of man's tools.

He was just a young, red-headed boy then, with bright hazel eyes. It would be a good many years until, an experienced farmer himself, he would see a way in which that simple, beautiful design might be improved to serve its purpose even better.

But that intent way of looking at things, which was his even as a boy, was what helped make Thomas Jefferson all the things he became—a man who would invent an improved moldboard for a plow one day, as well as write the Declaration of Independence; a man who would become an architect, a furniture designer, a scientist, and half a dozen other things, as well as a statesman and President of the United States.

He grew up in a time and place where there was much to encourage such an inquiring mind. It was 1743

14

when he was born—April 13th, to be exact. And in the middle of the eighteenth century, America was still a new world, even on the coast where the first settlements had been built. Inland, no farther than a hundred or a hundred and fifty miles, there was still real wilderness, where everything was strange and unfamiliar to all men but the Indians.

The real wilderness rose just beyond the cleared fields of Shadwell, the farm in western Virginia where Thomas Jefferson was born and spent most of his boyhood.

And the wilderness fascinated young Thomas almost as much as the plow that tamed it.

How old must those trees be, to grow so tall?

What was that animal, peering from the thicket? Or

that one, whisking away through the trees?

What sort of life did the Indians live in these forest deeps? Why were they always roaming, never settling down as the white men did?

He was fortunate, this curious boy with the eager eyes and the out-thrust, stubborn chin. There was a whole, bright new world spread out around him. And he had a father who welcomed all his questions about it, answering the questions when he could, urging the boy on to answer them for himself whenever possible.

In many ways that father, Peter Jefferson, set the course for young Thomas' life.

Peter Jefferson was truly one of the strong men of early America, a pioneer who broke the wilderness and carved out a vast and profitable estate for himself and his family, and at the same time, a man who was constantly seeking to educate and improve himself intellectually, a man always ready to serve his friends and neighbors in any way he could.

He was a giant of a man, physically, and had personally helped clear a thousand acres of virgin forest to create the cleared fields of Shadwell and build a home. He was so strong that Thomas would watch and marvel as he flexed his muscles and pushed upright two 1,000-pound hogsheads of tobacco at one time. Another time Thomas saw his father give a mighty tug at a rope with which three strong slaves had been trying to pull down a shed, and bring down the shed in a heap.

16

". . . the cleared fields of Shadwell"

Of course, Thomas wanted to be as strong as his
father. His eyes intent, his chin set, he threw himself
into learning all the physical skills his father was eager
to teach him. He learned how to ride a horse, how to
handle a gun and hunt, how to paddle a canoe on the
swift, rock-strewn waters of the little Rivanna River that
ran through the Shadwell lands.

And year by year, as Thomas grew taller and taller,
he did grow lean and strong, with a physical endurance
that would last all through a long, long life.

"Never," Peter Jefferson told his son, "never ask

anyone else to do for you what you can do for yourself."

So Thomas learned the habit of doing all sorts of things for himself. He learned how to do things which, perhaps, there was no need for him to do, since there were slaves aplenty at Shadwell. But somehow that advice of his father's came also to mean, "Never ask another to do what you are not willing and able to do yourself."

The plow was not just a tool for others to handle. Thomas himself had to learn how to use that tool, driving a straight furrow across the field. And because a farm at the edge of the wilderness, in the eighteenth century, was a little world in itself, Thomas learned dozens of other skills as well.

He learned about spinning and weaving and dyeing. He learned about wagon-making, brick-making and nail-making. He learned about distilling, and caning chairs and shoeing horses. All these activities were part of the busy life of Shadwell, carried on in sheds and outbuildings clustered all about the main house; and so they were part of Thomas' life, too.

But his father, who had found for himself the world of books, his father, who loved Shakespeare, and Swift and Pope, wanted more for his son than a knowledge of physical skills. Thomas was still very young when his father taught him how to read and write and keep accounts. Soon he was exploring the library at Shadwell.

Books were one thing that could not be produced

18

on even the most self-sustaining of farms. Books were treasures, brought from the coast, where they had been imported from Europe. Books were the first thing one thought of buying when it came to a question of spending cash for something.

Books first, and then perhaps musical instruments. People had to make their own music in those days, and Thomas, who loved it, soon learned to play on the fiddle. It was an accomplishment that would bring him pleasure all his life.

Indoors, outdoors, there was always something to learn. But above and beyond everything else in those years, there was something more Thomas was gaining as he watched his father. It was a vision of man as a builder—man clearing the wilderness to build a useful, productive farm; man using and sharpening all his talents to banish chaos and confusion and create order.

He was only six when his father, a self-taught surveyor, rode off with a professor from William and Mary College, which was over on the seaboard, to survey and map the still uncharted areas of western Virginia. His father and the professor came back with the first map ever compiled of "The Inhabited Parts of Virginia."

So Thomas saw that beyond the reach of the axe and the plow, man could still push back the unknown by exploration and observation, laying the foundation for future building by others.

Order—finding it in nature, creating it where it did

not exist—this was man's goal in life. In order, there was room for his own talents to increase and expand, for everyone's talents to have their fullest scope.

And what was the way to that kind of order? For Thomas, the first step would always be: asking questions.

Shadwell bordered the wilderness, but there were a few neighboring farms all the same. There was a tiny town nearby, called Charlottesville. And there was a little Latin School near Shadwell, held in a small log house and presided over by an elderly clergyman.

Here, when he was thirteen or so, Thomas began to learn Latin and Greek and higher mathematics. Here he also met a friend, Dabney Carr, almost as curious about everything as he was.

Now, when school was out and Thomas went off hunting or exploring in the forest, Dabney Carr often went with him. Together they would spy a fox or a bird.

Where was its den? Where was its nest?

Silently, trying to walk like Indians, they would track the fox or bird, find the den or the nest, study it, and ask themselves why and how it had been built just so.

Then, one day, as they were wandering on one of the hills that lay across the Rivanna, they made a wonderful discovery. They had climbed a long, rough way through virgin forest, and at last they came out on the top of the hill. And both of them stopped and stared.

Latin School

It was not the highest hill anywhere about, but somehow from this hilltop they had a view like none they had seen before. The whole world seemed spread out below them, hills and valleys rolling endlessly to the horizon both east and west.

They were silent a moment looking. Then the majesty of it all so overwhelmed young Dabney he could think of only one response grand enough. He told Thomas that here, on this hilltop, was where he wanted to be buried when he died.

"... a view like none they had seen before"

Solemnly, Thomas nodded in agreement. He wanted to be buried there, too.

Then Thomas had a less sombre thought. This was more than a place to be buried. This was a spot on which to live.

"This is where I am going to build my house one day," he said.

Dabney looked at him. "A house—here? On a hilltop?" Nobody built houses on hilltops. Houses were built in the lowlands, by rivers or streams, so that crops of cotton, corn or tobacco would have easy transport to the coast.

But "Why not?" asked Thomas. His father had built a house in the wilderness, where no man had built before. Why should he not build on a hilltop? There would be ways to solve the problems. He would figure out

22

ways. Because, as he stared out over the rolling hills, he felt sure that no one could ever be or think anything mean or small up here. Every thought must surely be tempered by this great vista into goodness and beauty.

"Yes, this is where I will build my house," said Thomas.

II.

AND SO, WHAT IS A HOUSE? AS THE DAYS AND WEEKS AND months went by, this was a new question turning itself over and over in Thomas' mind.

First of all, of course, a house is a shelter of wood or stone or brick, to keep a man and his family warm and dry against the elements.

But Thomas knew already that a good house was more than that. A good house provided comfort and convenience as well as shelter. A good house held the people within it in friendliness, offering them rooms in which they might enjoy themselves together, other rooms where they might be alone. He looked at his own home and knew Shadwell was a good house in that sense, full of affection and activity, its doors always open to guests and visitors.

But somehow Thomas wanted something even more for his hilltop.

A good house should be beautiful, too, he thought. It should fit the land on which it was built and express the dreams of the person who lived in it.

Where had this idea come from? Partly, perhaps, from the books he read, but mostly from his own heart. For Thomas was already that unusual combination—a practical person, methodically concerned with how everything worked, yet full of a passionate sensitivity that saw beyond all those details to some great ideal of beauty.

He wanted a *beautiful* house. But where, Thomas wondered, would he ever find a house beautiful enough for his hilltop? Or one that would express all that he felt when he stood there?

The days of his boyhood went on.

And then, when he was fourteen, his father died. That mighty man, the polestar of his youth, was gone.

Thomas was head of the family now, responsible for his mother, his younger brother, his six sisters.

Because he was the oldest son, all of Shadwell was his, too, including the hill where he meant to build his house. His younger brother was willed other farms from Peter Jefferson's holdings—for Peter Jefferson had not held with the general custom of those days in Virginia whereby a man left all his land for his oldest son. He did not believe in this, and one day Thomas himself, spurred as always by his father's example, would take real steps to abolish the custom in Virginia completely.

24

Right now there was nothing to do but accept his inheritance, go on with his studies, and try to carry on the Shadwell pattern as his father had established it.

Two guardians had been appointed to advise him till he came of age, but in actual fact, it was Thomas who had to supervise the day-to-day activity of the farm and give orders to the overseer. It was Thomas who had to carry on his father's tradition of lavish hospitality. Guests were always being entertained at Shadwell— neighboring squires and farmers; any travelers or hunters who might be passing by; Indians, too, with whom Peter Jefferson had always been friendly.

Young Thomas enjoyed the guests, and the Indians were his friends. He talked with them all, eager to find out everything he could about their customs and laws and habits. Already he was interested in learning the Indian language.

"What is your word for that?" he would ask a bronzed guest in buckskin, pointing up to the sun. Or he would ask the word for rain, or snow, or clouds.

He knew quite a few words of Cherokee, but different tribes spoke different languages. He was curious to learn the different words that referred to the basic, natural elements. Perhaps there might be some similarity in them that indicated they were all just variations of some common language. Or perhaps, way, way back, they were all based on some known language.

There was a theory about in those days—Thomas

heard some of his neighbors discussing it—that the Indians were originally the ten lost tribes of Israel, and had wandered to America somehow, by way of Asia. This did not seem very likely to Thomas, but a study of all the Indian languages might give one some clue.

All sorts of questions were piling up in his mind these days, dozens of questions for which no one seemed to have any answers.

He was seventeen when it came to him that if he ever hoped to answer all of them he needed more learning than he could get from the old clergyman, or even from reading by himself. Besides, all the activity of the farm, with the guests coming and going, kept him from studying as much as he would have liked.

He decided to leave home and go to college.

There was not much doubt about where he would go. William and Mary, one of the three colleges in exist-

ence in the colonies, was only a little more than a hundred miles away, in Williamsburg. It was so well thought of that students came from faraway New England to attend it, as well as from all over the South.

So young Thomas packed up his clothes and his fiddle and some of his books, and with his eyes brighter than ever, his chin tilted happily, he mounted his horse and rode off to Williamsburg.

What is a house?

In the rich and civilized little city he came to now, he saw many beautiful homes. There was the Governor's Palace, stately and dignified in red brick. There were other fine homes; George Wythe's for instance. George Wythe was a lawyer, renowned throughout the colonies, and his house, though simpler than the Governor's Palace, was large and gracious and well-proportioned.

Soon Thomas came to know both those houses well. A professor at the college, impressed by Thomas' eager intelligence, took Thomas under his wing and introduced him to both the Royal Governor and the famous lawyer. Soon Thomas, young as he was, was a close friend of the witty and able Governor Fauquier, the wise and thoughtful George Wythe. The Governor, the lawyer, the professor, and young Thomas were a foursome who met often for dinner at the Governor's Palace.

But the Palace, rich as it was, answered no dream

George Wythe's house

for Thomas of what his own house should be. Neither
did George Wythe's house.

Thomas was as popular with the young people in
Williamsburg as he was with the older men. He flung
himself at his studies as he had once flung himself at
learning to ride and hunt. Sometimes he studied as much
as fifteen hours a day, and then, for exercise, ran a mile
out of town and back again. With all that application,
and his own natural quickness, he was, of course, out-
standing. No one had ever seen a student who could
master so many different subjects so rapidly and so well

28

Governor's Palace, Williamsburg

—Greek and physics, calculus and Spanish, early Anglo-Saxon and Latin.

Still none of his fellow-students could bring themselves to resent his hard work or his success. When he put down his books, he flung himself just as eagerly into gaiety and liveliness.

His fiddle came out sometimes, as he played for his friends to sing or dance. He liked going to the theater when traveling players appeared in Williamsburg. He tried his hand at gambling. And he liked dancing, and flirting with the girls. He did not make many jokes himself, but everyone liked hearing his quick laughter when someone else said something amusing. His conversation was still full of questions, but his voice was so soft and mild, it was so obvious he really wanted to know whatever he was asking about, that nobody minded his endless curiosity.

Naturally, his popularity took him to balls and parties at all the fine houses in town, parties at nearby country houses, too. But none of these houses answered his dream either.

Two years Thomas persevered in college. Then he decided to take no more courses at William and Mary. He had made up his mind to be a lawyer. He would quit college and study law with his friend, George Wythe.

The law, he soon found, was nowhere near so much to his taste as some other subjects. But spurred by the example of his teacher, unable to do anything by half meas-

William and Mary College

ure, he flung himself at his law books. Of all the professions he might choose, he felt the law offered the most opportunities. So he would be a lawyer, and a good one.

Politics began to concern him. Sooner or later, everyone in Williamsburg was caught up in them. The House of Burgesses, to which his father had once been a delegate, met in Williamsburg, and Thomas often stopped in to listen to the debates when the House was in session.

The atmosphere was tenser now than in his father's day. Men were troubled by England's ever-increasing harshness in the rule of her colonies. A few tried to defend King George and his taxes, but more and more men were growing angry and defiant.

One day in 1765, Thomas was standing in the back of the hall when his old friend, Patrick Henry, rose to make the most violent attack yet on the King. "If this be treason," he concluded, "make the most of it."

Was it treason?

Of course, Thomas asked himself that question. Was it treason to suggest that if George III continued his despotic way, he might meet the same fate as other tyrants?

Asking himself that question simply led to other questions.

What were England's rights over her American colonies? What were the rights of any governing body over the people it governed?

Thomas pondered. He talked and argued with his friends. He read and he thought some more. And gradually, along with many other men, all over the colonies, he began to evolve answers for himself—answers that would one day startle the world.

Still, with all of this, the dream of the house was not forgotten. Summers, on vacation back in Shadwell, he would study all day, and then at sunset, he would paddle his canoe across the Rivanna to the foot of his own special hill. Then he would climb to the top and gaze out at the world that was visible from there.

He set some of the slaves he had inherited from his father to clearing the hilltop and leveling it off in preparation for the house he would some day build.

But still he did not know what that house would be like.

Then, one evening back in Williamsburg, he found out. It was his friend, Governor Fauquier, who helped give him the answer. Thomas was one of a group at the Governor's Palace and the Governor had some new books to show. One of them was a big, beautiful book of designs by a famous Italian architect of the previous century, Andrea Palladio.

Thomas took one look at the simple, classic lines of the buildings Palladio had designed and knew he had found the kind of beauty he was searching for. It was a house designed in this style that he wanted for his hilltop.

How would he achieve it?

Jefferson's sketch of Palladio drawing

III.

THERE WERE NO ARCHITECTS, AS WE KNOW THEM, IN THE colonies in those days, no one who could interpret those designs for Thomas into the kind of home he wanted.

Very well. Thomas recalled that his father had taught himself to be a surveyor. He, Thomas, would teach himself to be an architect.

He had learned some skill with a draftsman's tools from his father. Using Palladio's book as a guide, learning from every other book on architecture that he could find, he would design his own home in the Palladian style.

In the next few years, that is just what he did. He searched out every book on architecture in Williamsburg and hunted eagerly for more in every shipment from England. He sharpened his quill pen, tacked down paper on a drafting board, and made copy after copy of the precise and beautiful plates in Palladio's book. Finally, when it seemed to him he really understood the meaning and the reasoning behind the proportions and arrangements Palladio had used, he began to modify one of the plans and draw his own design.

It was 1767 when he finished his law studies and was admitted to the bar. He was ready to return to Shadwell and begin the practice of law in his home

county of Albemarle. He was ready also with his carefully drawn, carefully thought-out plan for a long, low, colonnaded mansion to be built on the crest of his hill. Monticello, he called that hill now, from the Italian for "Little Mountain."

There it was, his Little Mountain, rising green against the sky whenever he rode out from Shadwell or rode back again. But a young lawyer with a name and a living to make had little time to start on any project so grand as a mansion. One after another the cases came in. They took him all around the state to various county courthouses.

Still, he set the slaves to building a road through the forest up to the mountain top. And he began talking to everyone about a project that would certainly benefit a future house on the hill, just as it would benefit Shadwell and other farms along the Rivanna.

It was a project that had occurred to him a year or so before, on one of his vacations at home. Paddling up the little river, he began wondering if it were possible to clear it of the rocks which made any sort of transport so difficult. He had gone further, and surveyed the river, and decided that although it would be quite an engineering feat, it *was* possible.

So now he went from courthouse to courthouse with his cases, and from one person to another with his

The Rivanna River

scheme for clearing the Rivanna. By the time a year-and-a-half had passed, he had succeeded so well, both in his legal arguments and his river-clearance zeal, that he was elected to the House of Burgesses.

The first bill he introduced, however, had nothing to do with the river. It was a bill that proposed to give slave-owners the right to manumit, or free, their slaves.

He had grown up with slavery; it was part of the southern way of life, where vast tracts of land had to be kept in cultivation if the farmer was to see any profit. Still, almost as soon as he had started to ask questions, he had wondered how one man could *own* another.

Because a Negro's skin was a different color from the white man's, because he had been forcibly transported from his homeland to a strange country, did this mean he was not a human being, with the same rights as any other man?

He introduced the bill, the first of many he was to propose in the same cause, and it was defeated.

He had better luck with the river-clearance plan. Legislative approval was granted and soon the work was started that made it possible to send cargo craft, loaded with tobacco and other crops, down the Rivanna.

And what of his hilltop all this time? Was any progress being made at all toward fulfilling the dream?

There were some signs that someone planned to build there some day. And Thomas' memorandum book had other notations:

"four good fellows, a lad & two girls of about 16 each, in 8½ hours dug in my cellar of mountain clay a place 3 ft. deep, 8 ft. wide and 16½ f. long = 14⅔ cubic yds . . ."

And:

"in digging my dry well . . . they dug and drew out 8 cubical yds in a day."

And:

"Minor's sawyers left off work. They have sawed (as they say) 2500 pales, 220 rails. 650 f. of inch chestnut plank & 250 of 2¼ inch do."

And:

"A bed of mortar which makes 2000 bricks takes 6 hhds of water."

In other words, he had the start of a cellar and a well, timber had been cut and left to season, and he was beginning some sort of building.

But more and more legal cases were coming in. For all that he found the law cut-and-dried, Thomas was a success as a lawyer. He had twice as many cases the second year as the first, and his practice doubled again during the third year.

Yet the work on the hilltop went on. Thomas set out fruit trees to start an orchard for Monticello. He planted a few fields in various crops. A row of sheds was built on the hilltop, utility sheds to accommodate all the activities needed for building a house.

38

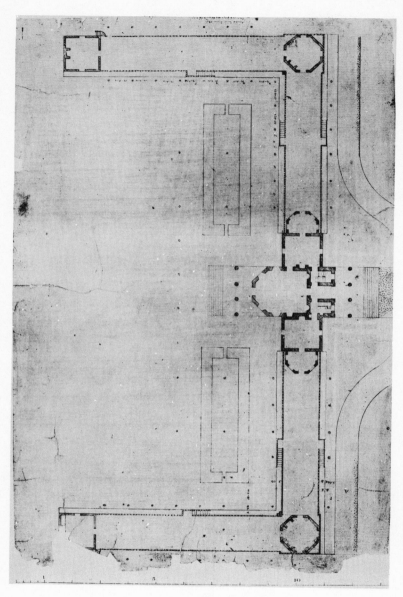

Jefferson's ground plan for Monticello

Finally, three years after he had come back to Shadwell, one small brick building was completed. In the grand, over-all design of Thomas' plan, it would ultimately be a small pavilion at the southeast end of one of the long wings stretching out from the central portion of the house. Thomas planned it for his office.

Then, in 1770, disaster struck at Shadwell. The main house burned to the ground. All Thomas' precious books were lost; the library he had inherited from his father and all the books he had collected so lovingly at Williamsburg. He would have to start buying books all over again, for life was no good without them.

But the fire left him in no doubt about where he should live. His mother and his sisters went to live in the overseer's house, but Thomas—Thomas went right straight up to Monticello.

"I have here but one room," he wrote to a friend, "which like the cobblers, serves me for parlor, for kitchen and hall. I may add for bedchamber and study, too. My friends sometimes take a temperate dinner with me, and then retire to look for beds elsewhere."

He had but one room, but at last he was living where he had vowed he would live, on his hilltop, with all the hills of Virginia spread out below him.

Two years more—two busy years as a lawyer with several months every winter and spring in Williamsburg when the House of Burgesses was meeting—and still there was only that one small building completed. Even

Martha Skelton Jefferson

so, Thomas was bringing a bride to live on the hilltop, too. He had found the love of his life, and on New Year's Day, 1772, he was married to the young and beautiful Martha Skelton.

Two weeks after the wedding, Thomas and his bride left her home, near Williamsburg, and set out for the Little Moutain. It turned out to be a dreadful day for the journey. One of Virginia's rare snowstorms had blown itself into a blizzard. Still, the new Mr. and Mrs. Jefferson struggled on. Before they reached Charlottesville they had to give up their snowbound carriage for horses. Then, as the horses floundered in the snow on

41

the slopes of Monticello, they gave up the horses, too, and fought the last distance up the hill on foot.

What is a house?

That night, when they were finally safe in the snug little red brick building, that one small room fulfilled the first requirement, giving them warmth and shelter against the storm. And with a fire in the fireplace, candles lighted and wine on the table, it was more than that too—a good house, however small, full of love and happiness and wonderful dreams for the future.

IV.

IT WAS THIRTY YEARS AND MORE BEFORE ALL THOMAS Jefferson's dreams for his house on the hilltop came true. But in the next few years, he did at least complete the main outlines of Monticello.

And in every part of it, it reflected the mind of its designer and builder, the man who saw everything as though it were brand-new, and asked himself how it worked, and if it could be made to work better.

The house consisted of a central pavilion, fronted by a portico, and extended on either side in two long ells. When it was finally completed it looked only one story high from the outside, and this was by design. Jefferson had never wanted a towering house on his hill,

Central hall at Monticello

but a house that looked as though it clung to the land, growing up from it like another long, low crest. Still, when one entered the main doors, the central hall rose in spacious two-story height.

The look of uncluttered space in this hall was no accident either. Jefferson had thought a long time about the problems of this main hall, asking himself first of all what its chief purpose was, then the other ways in which it would be used and how it could best be designed to serve those ends.

It was, of course, the room visitors would enter to gain their first impression of the house. It was also the room from which one went right and left to all the other rooms in the house, the room from which, most usually, a stairway would ascend to the rooms on the floor above.

But before Jefferson built his stairway, he remembered one of the chief uses of every central stairway he had ever seen. The occupants of the house used it. But even more than they, the servants were forced to use it in an unending parade of activity. Firewood had to be carried to the fireplaces on the second story, ashes brought down again. Hot water for bathing, cold water for drinking, food and dishes had to be carried up; jugs of water and dishes had to be brought down again.

Surely all the beauty of a wide, sweeping stairway was lost in the confusion of such traffic?

How, Jefferson wondered, could he do away with this nuisance, banishing all that needful, but distracting,

44

activity out of sight?

The answer he worked out was two small, sharply turning stairways on either side of the main hall, hidden away, leaving the hall itself free, open and beautiful.

He looked at other housekeeping problems and studied them as if no one had ever attempted to solve them before. The kitchen, for a large house like Monticello, was almost always in a small separate building near the main house. As a matter of fact, all the workshops of a large plantation were usually clustered about the main building in a random, haphazard fashion.

Jefferson had already banished these unsightly shops, offices and sheds, hiding them along the rear of the house, under a terrace. The kitchen was there, too. Even so, the food still had to be carried along an open walk to a warming kitchen and serving pantry inside the house.

Surely there was something that could be improved on here. Hot food lost its heat on this journey, and the servants were still exposed to all sorts of weather.

Jefferson decided to build an underground passage from the kitchen to the main house.

But this decision brought new problems. A tunnel would be damp. In the dampness, would the usual mortar hold the stones, or would it soon crumble away?

He began to experiment with mortar, using various proportions of lime and ash. Finally, after a dozen or more experiments, he hit upon a recipe which seemed to solve the problem perfectly.

He jotted down the proportions in his note book: "1 bushel each of lime, wood ashes, and pulverized brick, brought to the proper consistency will harden in water."

Actually, what he had arrived at, in those homely experiments on the hilltop, was an almost exact chemical foreshadowing of our modern formula for cement.

And so the underground passage was built and it is solid and dry to this day, almost two hundred years later.

Kitchen at Monticello

The underground passage was not the only innovation he thought of to make the serving of food more convenient. Before Monticello was finally completed, he had designed and built a service door to hang between the serving pantry and dining room. The door had shelves on the side turned to the pantry, which could be loaded with dishes and food. Then the door swung on a central pivot to bring the shelves into the dining room where they could be unloaded by the servants there. Naturally, it worked just as well in reverse, when it was time to clear the table.

Still another convenience was a small dumb waiter, concealed in the fireplace in the dining room. This dumb waiter went down to the wine cellar below, so that wine could be placed on it, and then drawn up into the dining room when needed. And, of course, the empty bottles could be returned the same way.

Other rooms in the house received his attention. There were large double glass doors between the main hall and the drawing room, and Jefferson worked out an intricate mechanism, concealed in the paneling, which caused one panel to open or shut automatically in harmony with the other as it was opened or closed.

He gave some thought to his own room, and how it might best be arranged for his own habits and needs. He liked to rise early in the morning and, after a cold bath, get to work at once on his notebooks or accounts. He liked to read at night, or answer letters before he

47

Chaise-longue and writing table

Dumb waiter

went to bed. His room, in other words, was as much a study and a workroom as it was a bedroom.

Was it necessary to have a bed, used only at night, taking up space all day in a room that was really a study?

He decided it was not, and designed a sort of double room with an alcove between the two halves. In this alcove, he had a bed hung on one wall, so arranged that it could be lowered at night, then hauled up and fastened against the ceiling during the day. The alcove passage became free when this was done, uniting the dressing room half of his room with the study in one airy unity.

And still he thought of more ways to make his house functional.

Years before real plumbing systems were invented, he evolved a plumbing system for Monticello, a way by which indoor privies could be emptied and the waste carried away, out of the house, and deposited underground in a central tank out on the grounds.

He achieved this by means of buckets, placed under the privy seats, which could be removed by a manually operated pulley, carried along an underground tunnel to the spot for emptying, and then returned, by pulley, the way they had come.

How does it work? How—if it has never been done before—can it be made to work? Asking himself these questions, there seemed no end to the improvements Thomas Jefferson could make in his home.

49

Jefferson's alcove bed

And there was always another question, too. How may it all be made as beautiful as possible, worthy of the hilltop?

Tall, graceful windows opened every downstairs room to the lovely views on every side, and opened the whole house to the cool airiness of hilltop breezes. Cornices, moldings and fireplaces were carved in simple, classic designs, and none was too hidden to be worked with meticulous care.

Every door was solid mahogany, every sash of solid walnut. The handwrought hardware was delicate and ingenious at the same time. Many doors had catches which engaged automatically as the door swung open and held it in place.

He had wonderful plans for the grounds surrounding the house—plans for formal gardens and a small Gothic temple, plans for wild life.

"Keep it," he wrote, while he was still planning, "in deer, rabbits, peacocks, guinea poultry, pigeons, etc. Let it be an asylum for hares, squirrels, pheasants, partridges, and every other wild animal (except those of prey). Court them to it, by laying food for them in proper places. Procure a buck-elk, to be, as it were, monarch of the wood; but keep him shy, that his appearance may not lose its effect by too much familiarity."

Oh, yes, he had hundreds of plans, and as the years went on, he kept thinking of new plans.

In the 1780's, a distinguished Frenchman came to America and visited Monticello, and when he went home again he wrote a description of the house which he ended by saying, ". . . we may safely aver that Mr. Jefferson is the first American who has consulted the fine arts to know how he should shelter himself from the weather."

But long before that visit was made, or those words

written, long before all the comforts and beauties just described were achieved, Jefferson had to stop his happy labors on the hilltop and leave his home for longer and longer periods.

The questions that had begun to agitate the American colonists back in the '60's were burning for answers now.

What *were* Great Britain's rights in the American colonies? Could the colonists win the King and Parliament to a less oppressive attitude by reason, or was there no alternative but revolt?

In 1774, men from all over the colonies were assembling to discuss those questions in Continental Congress. Jefferson was only thirty-one, but he had made enough of a reputation both as a lawyer, and in the House of Burgesses, to be named a delegate from Virginia.

At the last moment, illness forced him to stay home at Monticello. But he had written a paper outlining his own answer to one of the questions: "A Summary View of British Rights in America." The paper was read in the Continental Congress, and after that no one thought of Jefferson as an obscure young Virginian any more. He was a young man who obviously had ideas and knew how to express them.

In 1775, when the Second Continental Congress was assembling, Jefferson was again named a delegate.

He quit his house-building, said goodbye to his wife

and baby daughter, got into his carriage and started off. For the next few years he would be helping to design and build something even more basic and important than a house—a new kind of government that would try to take account of all the needs and desires of men as they had never been considered before, and then try to answer them in a better, more logical way than they had ever before been answered.

Handwrought ironwork

SCIENTIST AND NATURALIST

I.

ALL HIS LIFE HE WAS BUSY TAKING NOTES. HIS FATHER, who taught him so many things, started him on that habit also, and naturally, to anyone as engrossed as young Thomas in the how, the why, and the what of things, the habit was soon almost as automatic as asking questions.

There was always a notebook in one of his pockets. There were notebooks piled on his desk at home, and bundles of loose notes were tucked here, there and everywhere. He had an expense book from the time he first had money to spend. Later he began keeping a Farm Book, with notes on his planting activities and experiments and all his building projects. He kept a Garden Book with more notes on planting. And along with all these he had begun a Weather Memorandum Book, back in the Williamsburg days, in which he made regular entries on the weather.

Now, on his way to the Congress in Philadelphia, what else should he be doing during the long, slow journeying, day after day, but taking notes?

He sat in his light, open coach, jolting along over the rough, country roads, down from the hills of Virginia, out onto the flat, seaboard country of Maryland and Delaware, and finally, on across inlets and rivers to Pennsylvania. He propped a box on his lap to give him a writing surface and scratched away with his quill pen, taking notes on everything he saw.

As always, he was interested in the natural life all about him, the birds, the animals, the flowers, the trees. As always, he did more than note he had seen such a deer, or such an oak. He recorded the approximate size of the animal or tree, its coloring, its habitat, and every other distinguishing characteristic he could observe. He noted how the natural life changed with the changing countryside, how certain trees, familiar in the hills, were seen less and less in the lowlands, and how the same changes took place in animal life.

It was not a very comfortable way to write, sitting in an open phaeton, with the wind blowing his paper and the inkstand always about to overturn. But he kept on.

The changing weather from hill country to lowlands was something else to record. Weather study was a long way from being a science in those days, but all over the colonies, men of a scientific turn of mind were making observations on the weather where they lived, slowly charting some pattern for the climate of this great new continent.

The Fahrenheit thermometer was a recent invention, delighting men like Benjamin Franklin and Jefferson's old friend, Governor Fauquier. Jefferson had long since resolved to buy himself a new thermometer in Philadelphia. Meantime, he made notes on the clouds and rainfall, the sunshine and wind.

At night the stars interested him. Astronomical observation was something else in which Governor Fauquier had encouraged him.

And at night, stopping in various inns along the way, there were things to observe indoors as well. He paid for his supper and his bed, for lodging his servant and his horse—and one night the price was quoted in shillings, the next night in guineas, the next night in pistareens. There was no standard money system in use anywhere, and the logical, methodical Jefferson began to be annoyed.

56

Was a man supposed to carry a bagful of coins of every conceivable kind wherever he went?

He knew how the confusion had come about, of course. Men settled a new community and continued to use whatever money had been standard in their European homeland. Then as they moved about from settlement to settlement and men from different countries met, there was soon a hodgepodge mixture of a dozen kinds of coinages. It was understandable, but the whole thing was now ridiculous.

Just to show how very ridiculous it was, Jefferson

listed all the coins he had seen in use in his notebook. Then, of course, being Jefferson, he began asking himself questions.

How can the confusion be ended? What kind of coinage system would be best to set up as a standard everywhere?

In one corner of his mind he began thinking about answers to those questions right then. And the notes he took that spring of 1775 were seeds that flowered eight years later, when he became one of the Virginia delegates to a Congress of the newly independent states. By then he had a better money system all worked out and ready to present in a bill. The decimal system, based on units of ten, had finally seemed to him the simplest, most logical way in which to measure money values. He proposed a dollar unit in his bill, and a coinage system derived from that. And so he fathered the whole coinage system that we use in the United States today.

The notes he made on money were not the only seeds that flowered from the observations of that one particular trip.

Six years later, the notes he had made on flora and fauna, stars and soil, were to be of great value, too, when he embarked on a book describing the natural characteristics of Virginia. It became a book that won him fame both in America and abroad, and made him, as well, one of the pioneers of North American geography.

And that was still not the only consequence of those ten days' journeying from Monticello to Philadelphia. The inconvenience of his makeshift writing desk made him think how pleasant it would be to have a really well-designed traveling writing desk.

He sketched out a design—a compact box, not much larger than a big book, with a drawer to hold an inkstand and paper and quills, and atop it, a folding shelf which could be lifted and tilted as a reading stand, or opened out to use as a surface for writing.

It was a nice coincidence, after he had arrived in Philadelphia and found lodgings, to discover that his

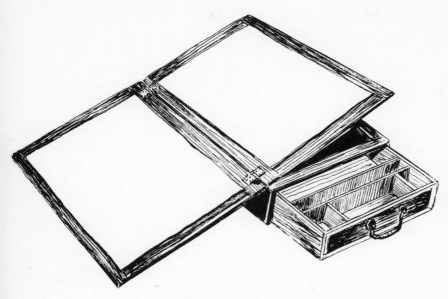

Portable writing desk

landlord, a certain Ben Randall, was a skilled cabinet-maker. Jefferson gave Ben Randall the sketches for the desk and asked if he could make up such a contrivance for him.

And so it happened that when he went home to Monticello in August, he carried with him a handsome and convenient little writing desk on which to take his notes.

Nothing had been finally settled in that Second Continental Congress. The conflict between England and her colonies had exploded into real fighting, at Concord and at Bunker Hill, but war had not been declared. New proposals from the King's chief minister had to be answered.

But a second session of the Congress was called for

the next June. And, again a delegate, Jefferson returned to Philadelphia, bringing with him the little desk—a desk that would soon be used for a most important writing assignment.

In this summer of 1776, the delegates were ready to make up their minds. They chose the tall, red-headed young Virginian to write out the announcement of their intentions—an announcement for England, and all the world to read—of the united colonies' Declaration of Independence.

Later, Jefferson said he had not tried to be original in writing out that Declaration, that he had simply tried to express the American mind. But if it was the American mind, it was surely Jefferson interpreting it. Simply, logically and beautifully, he was outlining the answers to the questions he, and so many others, had been asking.

What is the purpose of government?

"To secure men their inalienable rights to life, liberty and the pursuit of happiness." (The pursuit of *happiness*? What about the protection of property? There were many who felt this was the duty of government. But Jefferson had a vision of a government that protected all men, not just the lucky few. Every man had the right to pursue happiness and a good government would protect that right.)

How does any government derive its just right to power?

In the Declaration, Jefferson spelled out the simple

60

answer. A government derives its right to power "from the consent of the governed."

After he had written out his draft of the document on the little writing desk, he took it to the Congress. The delegates read it over and then began criticizing various passages.

Jefferson sat in silence, his firm jaw set. Criticism had always hurt him. Now, when it seemed to him he had weighed and pondered every phrase to make sure it was both exact and necessary, these arguments and disagreements over what he had written were like physical blows.

Worst of all was the disagreement about his words condemning the slave trade. Surely a document proclaiming every man's right to liberty should take a stand against an institution that denied liberty to some men because of their color!

So why? Why were some of the delegates who hated slavery as much as he did still insisting that passage be removed?

Deep in his heart, Jefferson knew why—knew why he himself kept the slaves he had inherited even though the idea of slavery appalled him. The southern way of farming was based on slave labor. Some new system for working vast plantations would have to be evolved before men would feel they could free their slaves.

Still, slave *trading* could surely be condemned?

But, no. The delegates crossed it out.

Wounded and unhappy, Jefferson still sat quietly—and went on taking notes, on the proceedings, and on other things as well.

On July 4, 1776, for instance, when the debating finally drew to a close, he noted in his expense book that he had spent 3.15 pounds for a Fahrenheit thermometer. And he also made a note of the temperature readings at various hours of the day. At 1 P. M. it was 76 degrees, a very pleasant and temperate day for the delegates finally to sign a document as explosive as the Declaration of Independence turned out to be.

II.

WHAT ONCE HAD BEEN COLONIES WERE STATES NOW. AND men from thirteen states were fighting the English in an effort to make good the independence they had declared.

As the two armies battled, Jefferson was fighting in another way. The states were free from Great Britain's rule in name only if their laws and institutions remained exactly the same. So back in Virginia, he was working in the House of Delegates to make the changes in Virginia's laws and Constitution which would really put the principles of democracy into action.

Years before, inspired by his father, he had begun

to be troubled by the old English law which provided that if a man died without a will, his estate be passed on, undivided to his oldest son. Another old English system, called entail, allowed one estate to remain undivided, and owned by the oldest male heir, forever. Now Jefferson realized that this system of entail and primogeniture actually created an aristocracy of landowners.

At last he had an opportunity to change this. He drafted and introduced and fought for the passage of two bills which abolished the two systems entirely. One allowed a landowner to will his estate to whomever he wished. The other amplified that freedom by giving him the further right to divide his lands however he wished and sell them to any purchaser he pleased.

Two more bills seemed equally important to him. One was aimed at distributing as widely as possible something even more vital than land. It was a bill providing for free public education. The other bill, which gave him the most satisfaction of all, guaranteed religious freedom to everyone in Virginia.

He was Jefferson, the Builder, laying the foundations of democracy in those days. He was Jefferson, the man who looked at everything to see how it might be made to work more efficiently, as he labored with his old friend and teacher, George Wythe, to revise Virginia's legal code.

But he was still Jefferson, the Scientist, taking notes

on all sorts of natural phenomena—the first blooming of the fruit trees at Monticello, the total eclipse of the sun in 1778, the uses of the *orrery,* a sort of planetarium which had just recently been invented.

In 1779, he was elected Governor and during his two years in that office there were troubles everywhere. The war was going badly both in the North and South; Richmond, the new capital of the state, was invaded, after which he himself was bitterly criticized by many people because the city had been so ill prepared.

Wounded as only he could be by this criticism, he was delighted when his term was over in 1781 and he could retire to Monticello to recover himself with all sorts of farming experiments.

For several years now, he had had a stimulating new neighbor, a certain Italian gentleman of many talents. Jefferson himself had induced him to settle nearby and experiment with growing wine grapes. Philip Mazzei was his name, and soon Mazzei was not only growing grapes, but had imported olive trees and sour orange trees as well.

Jefferson was growing some of these at Monticello, making careful notes on their progress. There were all sorts of other experiments underway as well.

And then came a scientific project that was really made to measure for him.

What was the state of Virginia like? What were its natural resources, its climate, its flora and fauna?

64

The French government wanted to know. A representative in the French legation in Philadelphia had forwarded the request for information to Jefferson.

Eagerly, Jefferson flung himself at the task of compiling the answers. Out came the bundled notes of years —all those notes he had taken on the journey to Philadelphia in 1775, notes he had taken on all of his journeys around the state, and on rambles over his own land— hundreds and hundreds of notes on trees and flowers, animals and weather, hills, rivers, rocks and stars.

For the next year he was working at arranging and

editing all these notes, and writing letters here, there and everywhere, for still more facts and statistics.

Some old bones had been dug up far inland, along the Ohio River. They were huge in size and the men who studied them had decided they belonged to some large quadruped they named a "mammoth."

Jefferson had been fascinated by the reports on those bones from the first moment he heard of them. Now he was busy collecting all the data he could get on them, to prove that the creature was indeed a mammoth and not an elephant as some far-off European scientists had tried to insist.

"A patient pursuit of facts, and cautious combination and comparison of them, is the drudgery to which man is subjected by his Maker if he wishes to obtain sure knowledge," he once wrote to a friend.

He called it drudgery, but he loved it all the same.

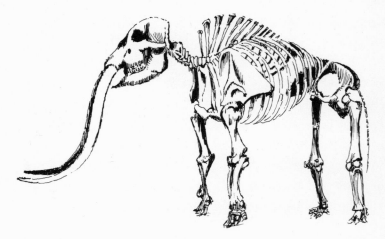

A mammoth

This was a book he had always wanted to write. More than that, it was a unique opportunity to set European scientists right, not only on the mammoth, but on all sorts of facts about America about which they were misinformed.

Notes on Virginia, he called it when it was finally finished and ready to send off to France. And in years to come it would become a classic.

But even as he was finishing the book, it seemed for a while as though all his interest in life were ending, too. It was the summer of 1782 and each day his wife, Martha, grew frailer and seemed less likely to recover from the birth of her last child. In September she died, and for months after that Jefferson was sunk in grief, roaming and riding the woods, speaking to no one.

At last it was his family that called him back to life again. He had three little daughters to raise. And there was a cluster of relatives living at Monticello, among them his sister, who had married Dabney Carr, and her children. (Dabney himself had died, and true to his boyhood promise, Jefferson had buried him on the hilltop.)

Suddenly, all these relatives and friends and all the slaves on the plantation as well, were threatened by an outbreak of smallpox, one of the most dreaded diseases of the time.

Smallpox! Now it was well indeed that Jefferson had always loved science, read about it, talked about it, corresponded about it with friends everywhere. Like a few

67

other people in America, he knew about innoculation against the disease. In fact, he had himself been vaccinated some years before in Phliadelphia.

But there were no doctors around Monticello who understood the process or had any faith in it. If his family and friends were to be innoculated, Jefferson himself would have to do it!

He reviewed all he knew about the process, remembering his own innoculation. He thought back over the letters he had received on the subject from scientists in England and France. And he got out all the medical books in his library and studied them.

Then, one by one, he innoculated each of his daughters, lightly scratching their small arms, rubbing in the fearful smallpox germs. One after the other, he innoculated the others, too. Then he waited for the reactions, hoping they would be no worse than headaches for a few days and sore arms.

It was all right! No one was really ill at all. Everyone had been saved from smallpox.

Later, when he was President, Jefferson was to throw all the prestige and authority of his office behind a movement to create general acceptance for an improved method of smallpox vaccination by means of cowpox. He did it with a conviction and enthusiasm that had been confirmed that fall of 1782, when he made his own pioneering effort in medical science.

III.

"A MIND ALWAYS EMPLOYED IS ALWAYS HAPPY." GRADUALLY now, with all sorts of mental employment, Jefferson began to be happy again.

He was a delegate from Virginia to the first Congress of the newly independent states, and among other bills, he was able at last to introduce his long-pondered bill to reform the coinage system. He proposed that weights and measures also be standardized to the decimal system, but this measure was defeated. Only his plan for standardizing the coinage was accepted.

Then, after just a few months, Congress asked him to go to France as a Minister Plenipotentiary, to assist John Adams and Benjamin Franklin in creating treaties with various European countries.

And so he went to France, where he was to remain five years, first in the original post, later succeeding Benjamin Franklin as Ambassador to that country.

He went, of course, on affairs of state for the United States, as a politician and a diplomat. But being Thomas Jefferson, he could not help going as a scientist and naturalist, and a farmer and an architect as well.

In all these roles, he had one chief goal—to observe and take notes and bring back as much information as

"And so he went to France . . ."

possible about everything in the Old World that would
be of value in the New.

But he had another aim also. He not only wanted
to learn. As an American, there were a few things he
wanted to teach Europeans, too.

All sorts of strange ideas about America were wide-
spread in Europe in those days. Jefferson had done his
best to correct them with facts and figures in his *Notes
on Virginia*, which was just about to be published in
France. But surely, going in person, there was even
more he could do, as he talked to people face to face.

There was one French scientist in particular whom
Jefferson wanted to meet, a certain Comte de Buffon,

pride of the French Academy, and one of the most respected authorities on natural history in the world. But
celebrated as he was, Buffon held one theory that irked
all Americans almost past enduring.

He believed, and published it for the world to read,
that all animals in the New World were smaller in size
than the animals in the Old World, that there were fewer
species there, and that animal and human life in general
tended to grow weak and feeble there.

Why were things in such a sorry state in America?
Well, Buffon blamed the climate, of which he knew very
little also. He said America's huge mountains and great
forests held an undue amount of moisture in the air,
that vast areas of the continent were covered with nox-
ious vapors and, as a result, all animal life suffered. He
believed, along with many other Europeans, that America really was a new continent, just recently heaved up
from the bottom of the ocean, and that nature had not
had time to finish the job there.

Even before he left America, Jefferson had been
thinking of ways to fight these fantasies. He saw a huge
panther skin at the door of a hatter's shop in Philadelphia, and bought it at once and put it with his luggage.
Here was proof, even more tangible than the facts and
figures in his book, that animals were anything but small
in America.

And of course he was going to talk a good deal
about that wonder of America, the mammoth. White

71

men had only seen its bones, but Indians claimed the huge creature still roamed at large in the wild northern parts of the country.

Oh, Jefferson had many things to tell French scientists, as well as many problems of state to help solve for his country.

At last, after he had been in France several months, he met M. Buffon. The scientist was amiable enough, but Jefferson found it very difficult to shake any of his convictions. "Read my book," the Frenchman said blandly, "and you will be satisfied that I am right."

Jefferson, his voice as mild as ever, but his stubborn jaw set, persevered. He showed M. Buffon the panther's skin and that made some impression. Then he discovered that M. Buffon was convinced no American deer had horns more than a foot long.

At once Jefferson was writing to a friend in America with an urgent request. Please, would he obtain the largest pair of buck's horns possible and ship them to him in France? Would he also send the skeleton and skin of an elk?

Some months later he received the horns, "a most precious present," but in the meantime he had been led into boasting to Buffon that the European reindeer could walk under the belly of an American moose. It was necessary to send a call back to America for the antlers, bones and skin of a moose.

It turned out that the order was not such an easy

one to fill. In the snows of a New England winter his friend went moose hunting, and after many misadventures, finally bagged one. Then there were endless problems in cleaning and arranging for the preservation of the skin. There were problems in transporting it to the coast, problems in getting it on board a ship for France.

At last, the dismantled moose arrived in Paris. Jefferson winced as he paid $150 in shipping charges, but soon he felt it had been money well spent. When M. Buffon saw the moose he was visibly shaken.

"I should have consulted you, Mr. Jefferson, before I wrote my *Natural History*," he said, and he promised to make various changes in the revised edition.

Buffon, of course, was not the only scientist with

73

whom Jefferson talked or corresponded. His scientific missionary work ran through all his busy days that were filled with ambassadorial duties and other political responsibilities.

Back home in the United States, an earnest group of men was laboring to write a constitution for the new nation. Jefferson could not help wishing desperately that he were there with them, helping to create this uniquely important document. Next best to being there was to write constantly to his friends in the constitutional convention, filling his letters with all sorts of suggestions about ways in which to insure a truly democratic constitution. He scoured the Paris bookstores for books on government, and shipped them back to his friends.

Still, he always found time for letters correcting misstatements about America which he found in foreign encyclopedias and books. He always found time to meet with foreign scientists or write to them on the subject of the American climate, or American wild life. Whatever immediate effect all his efforts had, he undoubtedly played a part in bringing European scientists a truer picture of America than they had had before.

And meantime, of course, he was always taking notes—notes on all sorts of European advances in the fields of science, or invention or agriculture; notes on everything he thought would be of value back home.

One of the most exciting advances of the day was man's first conquest of the air, by means of balloons. In 1783, just before Jefferson went to Paris, the Montgolfier brothers had given the first public demonstration of the lifting and flying properties of a balloon.

By the time Jefferson was living in France, ballooning was the rage and he wrote many detailed reports on the balloon demonstrations he witnessed. Of course,

Paris bookstores

being Jefferson, he also speculated on the future useful-
ness of ballooning to mankind—the way in which air
travel could transport commodities over difficult or enemy
territory, the way in which ballooning could be used
to throw new light on atmospheric phenomena. He even
suggested that the Pole might be discovered by air
flight, a project that ice had always made impossible
by land.

He made a visit to England and took notes on fac-
tories and steam mills there. "A peck and half of coal,"
he noted, would do "exactly as much as a horse" could
in a day. He speculated that the steam engine principle
applied to boats would "lay open all the streams to
navigation," and he felt a surge of satisfaction that
America had so much coal.

Back in Paris he watched a demonstration on the
Seine of a boat crossing the river, propelled by a screw
turning in the air. He wrote home about this invention
and suggested that it might work even better if the
screw were in the water.

All the latest scientific publications intrigued him.
He bought them and sent many of them back home, to
friends at William and Mary, at Yale and at Harvard.
And he wrote to other friends about the latest discoveries in astronomy.

In the midst of all this, he fell and broke his wrist.
It was a painful fracture and it was not set properly.
Worst of all, it was his right wrist. Slowly, painfully,

Along the Seine

his jaw firm, he taught himself to write with his left hand.

Then in 1787, he took a three-month tour of southern France and northern Italy. Never mind the difficulty in writing now! A positive blizzard of notes flew from his pen as he jotted down facts and figures about bridges, gardens, pumps, plants, forges and everything else he saw that seemed as though it might be useful in America.

During this trip, Thomas Jefferson, Architect, appeared again, too. From the beginning of his stay in Europe he had delighted in seeing for himself the architectural beauties of the past which had been known to him only through books before. Now, in Nîmes, the site of many Roman ruins, he fell in love with a beautiful classic building known as the Maison Quarrée. He spent hours gazing at it and sketching it.

Ultimately those sketches of the Maison Quarrée became the basis of his second big architectural project, a project he carried out while still in Europe. Friends in Virginia wrote him and asked him to find an architect to design a new state capitol for Richmond. He found an architect, all right, but what that other architect did is hard to know. It was Jefferson's design, based on the Maison Quarrée, which was sent back to Virginia and which was used to create Richmond's beautiful new capitol building.

Maison Quarrée, Nîmes

Capitol building, Richmond

But all the while, wherever he went, it was every aspect of farming that interested him most. He thought of America as a country which would always depend more on her farms than on any kind of industry, and he was sure that farming was the happiest way of life there was, both for a man, and a country.

"The greatest service which can be rendered any country," he wrote, "is to add an useful plant to its culture; especially, a bread grain; next in value to bread is oil."

79

So he took notes on dozens and dozens of European plants that he thought might be adapted for American culture, but he felt his greatest enthusiasm for the olive tree and a certain kind of rice that grew in Italy.

He had already experimented with the olive tree back in Monticello, thanks to his friend, Mazzei. But there were new varieties to observe in southern France. He arranged for some of these to be sent to America. Perhaps they would do better than the ones already there.

As for the rice, he had read of a species growing in northern Italy which was supposed to be far superior to the American Carolinian variety. He wondered if that superiority might be due to an improved cleaning machine, but naturally, he had to see for himself.

Jefferson began asking questions about rice as soon as he arrived in northern Italy. Finally, in the area of Vercelli, he found the grain he was looking for.

He studied the cleaning machine. It was identical with the ones used in America. Plainly it was the rice itself which was better. Plainly this rice must be tried in America.

But then came a horrid discovery! There was a law against exporting any of this rice from the Piedmont region of Italy. It was, in fact, a crime punishable by death.

Thomas Jefferson reflected a while. He had a great respect for the law, but an even greater respect for reason. It had never seemed reasonable to him for a few men to keep for their own exclusive pleasure or profit something that would benefit all men, whether it was land, or freedom, or education—or rice.

He decided to break the law.

Quietly he looked about until he found an obliging muleteer, who agreed to carry two bags of the rice over the Apennine Mountains to Genoa, where Jefferson would soon be going himself.

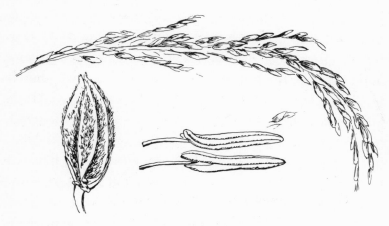

Rice plants

Then, just in case, Jefferson filled his coat pockets with some more of the rice and pleasantly took his leave.

It was a good thing he took that last precaution. In Genoa, he waited vainly for the muleteer to arrive. So it was the rice he had taken in his pockets that was sent back to America, where, incidentally, it grew very well indeed.

81

As for Thomas Jefferson, Smuggler, when he looked back on the whole business he felt nothing but satisfaction. In fact, he sometimes felt his importation of the Italian dry rice to America ranked with his authorship of the Declaration of Independence as a contribution to his country.

1787. 1788. The years in Europe were going by, and for Thomas Jefferson, the scientist, the farmer, the architect, the art lover and the book lover, they were full of all sorts of discoveries. But still he was growing homesick for his hilltop in Virginia. Only two daughters were left to him—Martha, called Patsy, and Maria, known as Polly—and both of them were with him. Still, he yearned for home.

The arts and sciences of Europe intrigued him, but the tyranny of almost every government in Europe was appalling to him. Nowhere but in America did men have any voice at all in how they would be governed.

1788—and he beguiled the spring with another trip, this time through the Low Countries and western Germany. Again there was a storm of note-taking, sketching and letter-writing. In Holland he saw a new sort of plow which he studied and sketched. He made notes of a machine for drawing empty boats over a dam. He admired and sketched various bridges.

Various household conveniences in Holland impressed him. There were windows designed to open so as to admit air and not rain. There were tables which would let down "with single or double leaves so as to take the room of their thickness only with a single leaf when open." These he sketched, too. And in Germany he was impressed by an invention which would one day become a household institution in his own country, central heating.

But the longing to be home kept growing.

1789. In Paris Jefferson heard that the new Constitution of the United States was going into effect in March. In April, George Washington was being inaugurated as its first President. The revolution which had begun to rack America in the 1770's was over and a new government was born.

From Paris Jefferson wrote to his old friend, the new President, and begged for a leave of absence from his post to visit home for a while.

The answer was slow in coming. Before it arrived, France's own revolution had begun its terrible course with the storming of the Bastille. Thomas Jefferson, Democrat, who had been observing the wretchedness of the poor French people for years now, might recoil at the horror, but he could only sympathize with the desperate need of these people for a better life.

The Marquis de Lafayette and other French friends came to him asking his help in framing a new Constitution for France which might help avert further disaster.

83

"He set sail for America"

But Jefferson was a foreigner, in a delicate diplomatic post. Once again he could only sympathize, and offer his ardent wishes for their success.

And then, at last, word came from President Washington, granting him a six-month leave of absence from his duties in France.

In October, he and his daughters set sail for America, along with eighty-six packing boxes, fifteen of them filled with books. Others held art objects, paintings, sculpture, models, and, of course, scientific instruments and curiosities of all kinds. He was taking back also the seedling of a cork tree, various other seeds, plants and cuttings—and to round out the luggage, there were a couple of shepherd dogs as well.

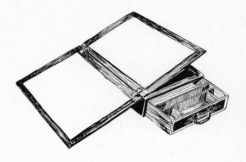

INVENTOR, ARCHAEOLOGIST
AND EXPLORER

I.

INVENTIONS! NEW COMBINATIONS OF KNOWN FACTS, NEW
techniques for doing things—Thomas Jefferson had been
fascinated by such matters from the time he was a boy.

And so it was a nice stroke of fate that made him
the first man in charge of granting patents from the
United States Patent Office.

How did that happen?

It happened because the patent office had been put

under the authority of the Secretary of State. And no sooner had Jefferson returned to Monticello from France than George Washington wrote to him, asking him to serve as the United States' first Secretary of State.

So there were only a few weeks on his hilltop after all. There was time enough to visit all the familiar haunts, time enough to see Patsy married to her handsome second cousin, Thomas Mann Randolph, whom she had long adored. There was time to worry about the way the farmlands had run down in his absence, and to ask Thomas Randolph to manage things for the next few years. Then he was off for New York, the temporary capital of the nation.

Now began three of the most hectic and troubled years in all his public career. Alexander Hamilton, Washington's Secretary of the Treasury, was Jefferson's great adversary during these years. It seemed to Jefferson that Hamilton's sympathies lay completely with the rich, and that he was trying in every way to ally the interests of the wealthy with the interests of the new government. Surely the colonies had not fought with England and struggled to create a new nation simply to put the rich in power again! Jefferson set his jaw, lined up all those who shared his own ideas of democracy, and opposed Hamilton in every way he could, with every counter-attack he could devise.

Even so, he took his duties as head of the Patent Office very seriously. And just as he felt that the new nation had been created to benefit everybody, not the rich alone, so he felt that the chief value of new inventions lay in their becoming available and useful to everyone, everywhere.

He had great respect for real inventors and he wanted them to be suitably rewarded for their originality, but he was even more anxious to make sure that a patent would never grant anyone an unlimited monopoly, which could hold back the progress of other inventors and Americans in general.

He favored a patent that would last for only a certain specified length of time, and before a patent was granted on any device or technique, he wanted to make sure that it really did add something new and useful to the world.

In spite of all his other worries, cares and duties, Jefferson personally examined every invention brought to the Patent Office. When he was the least bit in doubt about the worth of any particular device, he called in experts to advise him. Often they were fellow-members of the American Philosophical Society in Philadelphia. The word "philosophy" in Jefferson's day had a somewhat different meaning from now. Philosophy embraced all branches of learning, but most especially it was used to mean scientific learning. So these gentlemen of the Philosophical Society were among the most diligent and informed scientists in America.

The first patent Jefferson granted, in 1790, was to a certain Samuel Hopkins of Vermont, for a "process of making pot and pearl ashes." These products, derived from leaching plant ashes with water and then evaporating the solution in iron pots, were widely used at that time, and until the middle of the nineteenth century, in the process of making glass. Obviously, Jefferson was convinced that Mr. Hopkins of Vermont had devised a better method than the one in general use for making these ashes.

But he called in his advisors from the Philosophical Society when a man brought him a new method for obtaining fresh water from sea water. He was not easy in his mind about it.

The scientists watched the demonstration carefully and gradually realized that the so-called "new" system was simply the old and well-known method of distillation, camouflaged by some fancy hocus pocus.

The man did not get his patent.

However, when a man named Eli Whitney demonstrated a new machine for cleaning cotton, Jefferson saw at once that here was indeed a brand-new and extremely useful technique for dealing with one of the biggest problems in cotton growing. The patent was granted.

Jefferson's interest in Eli Whitney continued through the years. He was intrigued, later, when Whitney demonstrated that muskets did not have to be made one by one, each part being carefully and individually crafted for each new gun. Instead, Whitney had a number of identical parts made, arranged them in piles, and showed that a musket could be assembled using one part from one pile, one from another, and so on. It was the first practical demonstration in this country of the technique of interchangeable parts and mass production, and Jefferson recognized it immediately as a system that could be of immense benefit in many kinds of manufacturing.

But for one true inventor like Eli Whitney who came to him, there were dozens like the tricky distiller of sea water, and dozens more whose brain children were of no practical value to anyone.

As a result, in his three years of administering the patent laws, Jefferson only granted thirty-seven patents. A good many people were aggrieved by this strict attitude, so when Jefferson resigned as Secretary of State, and gave up control of the Patent Office, they raised a storm for the conditions to be made easier.

The law was changed to allow for the granting of patents without an examination.

Naturally, this soon led to the wildest kind of confusion, and before too long, the law was revised again, closer to the form that Jefferson approved.

Meantime, Thomas Jefferson, the inspector of other men's inventions, was also busy as an inventor himself.

He had come back from France with an idea in his head, an idea that had been born from some of his observations in Europe. Off and on, during his years as Secretary of State, he devoted some time to working out this idea.

He had always been fascinated by the plow and in

90

Europe, wherever he went, he had paid particular attention to the different kinds of plows that were in use. In Germany and in France, his eye had been caught by the awkward figure of the moldboard on the plows he saw.

What is a moldboard, basically?

"The offices of the moldboard," he wrote in his notes, "are to receive the sod after the share has cut under it, to raise it gradually, and to reverse it. The fore-end of it then, should be horizontal to enter under the sod, and the hind-end perpendicular to throw it over; the intermediate surface changing gradually from the horizontal to the perpendicular. It should be as wide as the furrow, and of a length suited to the construction of the plough."

As always, he was looking first to understand the purpose. Then he was ready to think of how that purpose might be better served. He was ready to make diagrams to show precisely how a moldboard might be cut from a solid block of wood to serve its purpose much

Jefferson's plow

more efficiently than before.

He made the diagrams; he corresponded with his new son-in-law, Thomas Randolph, about the idea; finally, he even had a small model made.

But it was not until he had retired from office and returned to Monticello in 1793, that he was able, at last, to have a plow made according to his design.

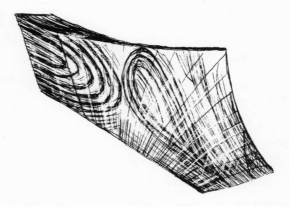

Moldboard

He tried out the plow with its new moldboard on his own fields and was delighted with the results. It worked beautifully, increasing the efficiency of the plow immensely.

But not for Thomas Jefferson any patents on his own inventions. "All the world is welcome to any useful idea of mine," he said. He began at once to demonstrate his new plow to farmers around about in Virginia, and he gave them the design of his moldboard so care-

92

fully detailed that any carpenter could make it up without a mistake.

He wrote about his new invention to those who were too far away to see it in use and sent them models and drawings of it. A model was ultimately sent to France where it was not only much admired but won for Jefferson a gold medal in France's Society of Agriculture. But to Jefferson, the best reward of all was the fact that many copies of his plow were in use, helping farmers here, there and everywhere, to plow more productively.

II.

HE HAD RESIGNED AS SECRETARY OF STATE. HE HAD GONE farther than that. He said to everyone that he was through with politics forever. From now on he was going to devote all his time to his real delights, science and reading and farming.

His head was full of agricultural projects. During the years he had been away his acres had become less and less productive. The soil was exhausted by constant crops of tobacco. But Jefferson had observed a new method of planting while he was in England—a system of crop rotation.

Now he became one the first farmers in America to try this new system of planting. He experimented with various crops in rotation, making careful notes in his Farm Book as to which plantings most enriched the land.

"1. Wheat, followed the same year by turneps, to be fed on by the sheep.

"2. Corn & potatoes mixed, & in autumn vetch, the vetch to be used as fodder in the spring if wanted, or to be turned in as a dressing.

"3. Peas or potatoes, or both, according to the quality of the field.

"4. Rye and clover sown on it in the spring . . .

"5. Clover.

"6. Clover, & in autumn turn it in & sow the vetch.

"7. Turn in the vetch in the spring, then sow buckwheat & turn that in, having hurdled off the poorest spots for cowpenning. In autumn sow wheat to begin the circle again."

It was a slow process, taking many seasons before real improvement could be noted, but Jefferson was pleased and encouraged by the improvement that did take place.

Troubled by soil run-off after rains on plowed hills and slopes, Jefferson and his son-in-law also began to experiment with contour plowing. And in this, too, Jefferson was a pioneer, being one of the first farmers in America to try it.

Meantime, he worked out a new way of sowing clover from a seed box, rather than by hand, which cut down the time required for planting.

Not only plowing and planting but harvesting interested him. He was sure there must be a better way to thresh wheat than by having horses tramp on it in the open air on a threshing platform. When he was in New York as Secretary of State, he and another devoted farmer, George Washington, had once taken a special trip out to a farm where a new sort of threshing machine was in use. Together they examined it and speculated on its efficiency.

Now Jefferson became interested in a threshing machine which had recently been invented in Scotland. He had a model shipped to him and built a copy.

It worked extremely well, but, of course, being Jefferson, he soon saw some ways in which it could be improved. And, of course, once he had it working at top efficiency, he began urging all his neighbors to use this new system of threshing, offering them the use of his machine. Useful ideas were for everyone.

With all these improvements in farming methods, Monticello was still not making the profit it should. The Rivanna had long since been cleared and it was easy to ship crops down the river to Richmond or farther, but the prices paid for wheat and corn were sometimes discouragingly low. Jefferson began to think about some other ways to make Monticello profitable and decided to start a little nail factory.

One day in 1794, he noted in his Farm Book that "40 bundles of nail rods" had arrived. He assigned a certain number of his workers to this new project, and the nail factory was under way, turning out nails for purchasers all around the countryside.

Busy as he was out of doors, Jefferson was busy indoors as well. He had all sorts of projects for the house itself. There were improvements and alterations to be made everywhere. Certain architectural ideas he had observed in Europe had tempted him, and the low dome over Monticello's central pavilion was added now.

Then there was all that beautiful furniture, the paintings and art objects he had brought from France. These had to be arranged. There was curtain material he had bought in France, and that meant designing window draperies for various rooms.

Indoor activities stimulated his inventiveness as much as outdoor projects. Hours of reading and writing were part of every day's program. So now he thought of a new and convenient kind of chair. Instead of having to move his chair around when someone came into the room to speak to him, instead of having to get up to reach books or papers which had been placed off to one side, he would have a chair that swung around on its base.

He sketched a design for his swivel chair and had it built by Monticello's cabinet-maker. "Mr. Jefferson's

96

Interior of rooms at Monticello

Music stand

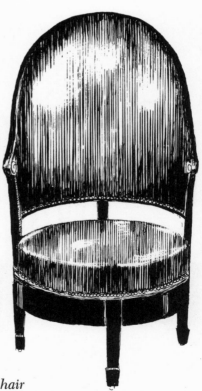

Swivel chair

whirl-i-gig" people would call it one day, but Jefferson only smiled and went on enjoying its comfort and convenience.

He had always loved music and musical neighbors often dropped in for an evening of playing chamber music. The little forest of music stands when four were playing set Jefferson's mind to speculating.

He designed a music stand which would hold the sheet music for four players, but with the music rests so arranged that they could be folded and dropped to make the stand equally convenient for three players, two, or just one.

He designed a clock for his front hall, the weights of which were cannon balls, and he added a further inventive touch by having it built so that the slow descent of the cannon balls indicated the days of the week, marked off, one below the other, on the wall.

Such a clock necessarily hung high on the wall. So he invented a collapsible ladder to be used for the weekly winding of the clock. Nor were any of these inventions vague ideas which he grandly passed on to someone else for the working out of details. He worked out the details, even for the intricate mechanism of the cannon-ball clock.

He worked out the details for yet another contrivance, this one an aid in his daily observations on the weather. He had a weather vane on the roof of Monticello attached to a dial in the ceiling of the front hall.

Jefferson's cannon-ball clock

An arrow on this dial indicated the direction that the weather vane was pointing outside. Now he did not have to step out of doors to take his daily notations on the direction of the wind.

Indoors, out of doors, his inventive mind was always busy looking for new ways to do things. New machines, new techniques, new conveniences—these were always his delight.

But he had an equal interest in things that were old. Classic buildings, beautiful old paintings, old books

Weather vane and compass at Monticello

—old bones, too. Years before, he had first become intrigued with the fossils men dug up from time to time in different parts of the country. The mammoth bones and other fossils gave fascinating clues as to what kind of animals once had roamed America, perhaps still roamed it in the wild regions to the west and north.

Now he had a special thrill as he himself came into possession of some bones belonging to an animal so far unknown to any American scientist.

III.

THE BONES HAD BEEN DUG UP IN A SALTPETER CAVE IN Greenbrier county, which is now part of West Virginia. They were shipped to Jefferson at Monticello, and as he unpacked them and spread them out on the floor, he felt all the excitement that always swept over him when a host of new questions challenged him.

What kind of animal had these bones once belonged to?

Those large bones there, with the huge claws—was it possible they were *toe* bones?

If so, what on earth was one to deduce about the animal's size? It must have been enormous.

Day after day, Jefferson pored over the bones, made notes about them and wrote long letters to his friends

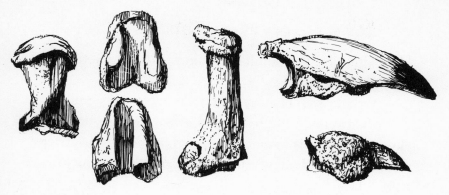

in the Philosophical Society about them.

But letters on another subject were coming in and going out, too, and had been for a long time. Jefferson made one tentative conclusion after another about his fossils, but all the while it was growing clearer that on this other subject he would soon have to make a hard decision.

The United States was having all sorts of trouble establishing itself firmly among the older nations of the Western world. There were difficulties in winning respect for its ships, its treaties, its rights.

After two terms, Washington was retiring as President, and without his unifying influence, two political parties had suddenly emerged on the scene. One was dominated by Jefferson's old enemy, Hamilton, and was committed to Hamilton's pro-British, please-the-rich policies. This group called itself the Federalist party, and had nominated John Adams to run for President. The opposition group, committed to Jefferson's equalitarian ideals, and sympathetic to the French Revolution, called itself the Democratic-Republican party. This party now was calling on its founder to come back into action and defend his principles.

At last, Jefferson agreed to run for President.

Meantime, though, he had also come to some conclusions about his fossils and he wrote these to his friend who was president of the American Philosophical Society. The bones, he had decided, "belonged to the family of the lion, tyger, panther, etc. but as preeminent over the lion in size as the mammoth is over the elephant." Still impressed by the toe bones with their huge claws, he suggested that this unknown creature be called "The Great-Claw, or Megalonyx," and he offered to give the bones to the Society for further study and for exhibit.

The president of the Society wrote back, much interested, and suggested that Jefferson write a full scientific paper on the bones. So now, as the election of 1796 loomed closer and closer, Jefferson was busily writing his first paleontological essay, describing his fossils and outlining his conclusions.

Then the election was held, the votes counted, and Jefferson's retirement was over. Those were the days when the candidate who received the most votes was elected President and the runner-up became Vice-President. Adams had received the Presidency. Jefferson was Vice-President.

It was goodbye again to Monticello, goodbye to the busy, happy hours in the fields, the happy, inventive hours indoors.

But he could not leave his fossils. He packed them up with his luggage and put them in his carriage as he started off to Philadelphia, then the nation's capital.

"Bones in his luggage!"

His political enemies were overjoyed when they heard that news. Science did not have the universal respect then that it has today. There were many people everywhere who felt that the investigations of science caused men to doubt the truths of the Bible. This, of course, was unthinkably sinful.

So the bones in the new Vice-President's luggage were not only a wonderful joke to spread up and down the land; they also gave his enemies new evidence that Jefferson was a dangerous, free-thinking meddler in all sorts of scientific speculation.

Jefferson was unperturbed.

"Almighty God created man's mind free," he said, over and over.

And if God had created it free, surely He meant man to use it freely, questioning, exploring, learning. No harm, no sin, could ever result from that, and one day, as the wilderness of ignorance and superstition gradually receded, everyone would realize it.

He was not too perturbed either when he learned that he had not been exactly right in the deductions he had made about his fossils. The discovery of bones similar to the Greenbrier fossils in other parts of the world had made it clear that this curious animal did not belong to the lion-class after all, as Jefferson had thought, but was a member of the giant-sloth family.

Jefferson knew that, for all his love of science, he was only an amateur and could hardly hope to be anything more. He made a note about the new discoveries in his essay on the fossils and deposited the bones with the Philosophical Society. The scientist-members accepted them gratefully, and in spite of his error in the

Megalonyx jeffersonii

classification of the bones, they decided to name the fossil for him—"Megalonyx jeffersonii."

And Jefferson's interest in bones and all the other antiquities of North America continued.

He was elected president of the Philosophical Society now, an office he would hold for many years. In this role, he sent out letters all over the country, urging men to be on the lookout for bones of unknown animals or any kind of relics that might be found in excavations or diggings.

He was also very eager for more serious exploration to be done in the vast, wild areas of the West. Many times through the years he had stood in his hilltop in

Virginia and looked out toward the western horizon, wondering about the unknown land that stretched on many hundreds of miles beyond his vision.

Did the mammoth still live and wander in those far-off forests?

Were there other huge animals there to further disprove Buffon's fantastic theories about American wild life?

And what of the Indian tribes to the west? Were there many of them? What languages did they speak? He was still adding to his notes on the various Indian languages, dreaming of some day compiling a dictionary of the Indian tongues.

Even before he became Vice-President, he had been urging the Philosophical Society to send an exploring party across the continent. Back in Monticello he had talked about it with his neighbors. An eager young fellow named Meriwether Lewis, who lived just a few miles away, had been so fired with enthusiasm that he volunteered at once for such an expedition. But for one reason or another, no such exploring party was ever sent forth.

It was not until four years later, when Jefferson himself became President of the United States, that he was really able to do something about the dream.

IV.

IT WAS A STRANGE ELECTION, THAT ELECTION OF 1800. But tense and dramatic as it was, Jefferson stayed calm. He was quietly writing letters about some mastodon bones that had just been dug up in New York, during many of the hours that Congress was voting to break a deadlock and determine whether he or Aaron Burr would be President.

Both parties had nominated Vice-Presidents this year, and Burr had been nominated for Vice-President on the Democratic-Republican ticket. But though that party had won handily, both Jefferson, nominated as President, and Burr had received the same number of votes.

Finally the long struggle in the Congress ended. The tie was broken. Jefferson was the third President of the United States.

In many ways, he was quite a different sort of President from the two who had preceded him. For a while he even seemed different from the Jefferson people had known before.

And that came about because once again he had been observing things and asking himself questions.

He had observed, for one thing, that during the last few years, the men of the new United States government were going farther and farther in their imitation of European royalty. Many thought that "splendor and pomp" were needed to create respect for the United States. Society in the new capital city of Washington, D.C., was becoming a courtly affair, full of protocol, trumpet flourishes and trappings of rank.

The old and the new. Jefferson loved what was good or useful or conducive to man's happiness in both of them. But to the bottom of his heart he knew this old-style emphasis on riches and rank was not good or useful or conducive to the general happiness in a country where democracy was the ideal.

How could he, as President, make this clear to everyone?

The answer was what seemed to change him, for a while, into quite a different sort of man from the one who had been such a delightful guest in the finest homes of Paris, the man who had always been such a gracious host at Monticello.

Suddenly, that Jefferson became a folksy, down-to-earth character who padded around the White House in carpet slippers, perfectly content to receive the most important visitors in any sort of old clothes.

He began the rule of "pelle melle" at White House dinners and parties. Nobody preceded anybody into the dining room or drawing room. Everybody just went in at random, taking whatever place was convenient or open.

It all caused a frightful scramble, of course, and

made a sensation that had repercussions in Europe as well as all over America. But Jefferson went calmly along his chosen way, refusing to give an inch to the stricken admirers of "good form." He refused to have his face used on coins, refused to have his birthday celebrated or even known. When he held an Open House at the White House, it was really open, and he would be as likely to spend his time with Indian chiefs as with important diplomats.

Then, when it seemed to him that he had made his point and made it impossible for society to pick up the old European patterns of behavior again, he quietly returned to the kind of dignity and graciousness that had always been his own true style.

110

Meantime, of course, while this experiment was going on, he really was the same Jefferson, pursuing his interests in science and invention and natural history in every moment not filled with the problems that faced him as President.

He was still experimenting with rice, trying to find a variety that did not require the watery condition of swamps for its culture. So he had twenty or more little pots of rice seedlings scattered about his Presidential office. There were pots of flowers, too—roses and geraniums—and two pet mocking birds to amuse and entertain him. One of them liked to perch on his shoulder while he was working or take food from Jefferson's own lips.

He had his kit of woodworking and metalworking tools at the White House and loved to tinker and make little things of his own design.

And, naturally, there were soon some bones in the White House, some exciting fossils unearthed in still another excavation. Jefferson spread these out for study on the floor of the still unfinished East Room.

Best of all, though, as President he was finally able to arrange for that long-dreamed-of exploring expedition to the West.

Young Meriwether Lewis had become his secretary during these years. Now Jefferson and the young man talked over plans for a journey that would follow the course of the Missouri River through the Louisiana Territory and then continue across the continent.

Then came the shocking news that Spain had ceded that same Louisiana Territory to France!

It was not his exploring expedition that Jefferson feared for. Actually, he went ahead and got secret approval from Congress for that venture, even though the Louisiana Territory now was the property of France. What alarmed him and alarmed all America, was the fact that France, a major power, now held the port of New Orleans, so vital for all shipping down the Mississippi River.

Jefferson rushed representatives to France with instructions to try to purchase the port of New Orleans. If they could achieve that, it would be a miracle, he thought.

He was unprepared—everybody was unprepared—for the fantastic purchase his representatives actually were able to make. They had bought the entire Louisiana Territory from France for $15,000,000.

Not everybody in America thought it was such a bargain. The territory was unreal and faraway. It took time for people to realize what a fabulous addition to the nation it was, doubling the United States in size, bringing it untold riches in natural resources.

But now there was no need for any more delay in the expedition that would explore this strange region. Young Meriwether chose a companion for the journey, William Clark, the younger brother of another Monticello neighbor, the Indian fighter, George Rogers Clark.

Jefferson briefed the two men with hundreds of questions he wanted to have answered.

Find out, he said, about the soil, the climate, the vegetation, the mineral resources.

Look for fossils and old bones.

Get acquainted with the Indian tribes across the country. Find out about their languages, their customs,

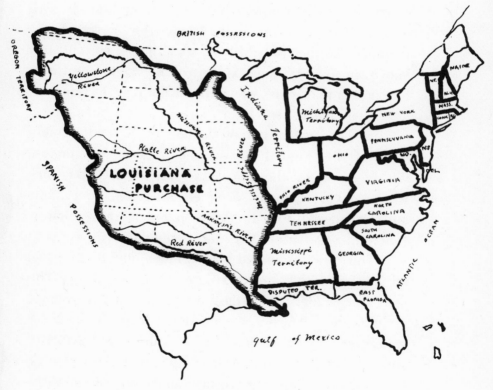

Map showing Louisiana Territory

their laws. And of course, he added, take them our friendship. He gave the two men vaccine to take along so that any Indians who might be persuaded to do so could be vaccinated against smallpox.

In 1804, they set off, two brave, resourceful and high-minded young men with forty-three companions. The journey before them filled Jefferson with longing. Since he was a boy he had loved exploring.

Instead, as they disappeared into the silence of the wilderness, the President had to content himself with long botanizing explorations along the banks of the Potomac, finding the thrill of something new and unknown in any strange leaf or tree he might see there, for "no blade of grass was without interest" to him.

Then, when Lewis and Clark had been gone almost a year, there was a flare of excitement. A small detachment of the original party came back to Washington with a report on the journey so far. Even better, they were carrying enough specimens of rocks, bones, furs and Indian weapons to throw Jefferson into a happy frenzy of observation and questioning.

The West fascinated him so much now that he sent off another expedition to explore for him by proxy. This one was headed by a dashing young captain named Zebulon Pike. It was Pike's mission to explore the head-waters of the Mississippi, the Arkansas and the Red Rivers, which he did. And it also happened that in the course of these travels, he found the peak in Colorado that now bears his name: Pike's Peak.

Finally, in 1806, Lewis and Clark themselves returned. And now, indeed, the wonders were really spread forth.

What was it like, that vast area of America stretching three thousand miles across forests, and prairies and mountains to the Pacific?

Now, at last, Jefferson, and all Americans could begin to find out.

As conscientious as they were brave, Lewis and Clark had taken enough notes to satisfy even the master note-taker himself. Their maps of the territory they had covered, the sketches they made, their observations on animals, vegetation and the country they saw, were so thorough and so extensive that they are still a national treasure.

In 1806, the story they told was like a revelation. It was real—all that land which people had only guessed about before! Its rivers, its mountains, its forests were real places, with names. The Indians who roamed that land were real people, too. Some of them had come to Washington with Lewis and Clark.

For the first time, men could think of actually traveling to those fantastic areas themselves, of setting up trading posts, even of living there.

As for Jefferson, he was turning the White House into a veritable museum as he displayed some of the trophies Lewis and Clark had brought back. There were antlers and Indian war bonnets, great chunks of minerals, furs and moccasins laid about everywhere. He was thrilled by these. He was even more excited by talking to the Indians who had made the journey east. His piles of notes on the Indian language grew and grew.

And out on the White House lawn the citizens of Washington, D.C., could now see two real live grizzly bears roaming around, the first grizzlies ever to be seen in the East.

"Jefferson's Bear Garden," his enemies began calling the White House, but Jefferson only laughed.

Through a lucky chance, he had been able to give his nation the Louisiana Territory. Through his emis-

saries, Lewis and Clark, the unknown was becoming known, the wilderness was being charted.

Why not bears on the White House lawn and war bonnets in the hall? What could better symbolize this brave, vast, strange country than such a mingling of the wild with the civilized, the old with the new?

V.

NOT ALL HIS PLANS AND PROJECTS WERE SUCH A SUCCESS.

There was little in the world that was alien to Jefferson, but war was one of those things. He was a man of reason, not of force and destruction. Even when war seemed necessary, as the Revolution had seemed, Jefferson had taken no part in the actual fighting, and his least successful public years had been as wartime Governor of Virginia.

Now war threatened again. Across the sea, England and France were fighting and that storm had eddies, drifts and cross-currents that were sweeping American ships and American trade into dangerous waters.

Would the United States have to fight England again to protect her ships and commerce?

There were many who thought so, many who wanted nothing better.

But Jefferson wanted no part of it. Surely, he thought,

there must be some way to protect American interests without that. Besides, the United States was totally unprepared for war.

So he forced Congress to pass an act which prohibited American trade with any of the warring nations. It was an act which, in effect, took United States ships off the high seas entirely. This would keep the United States out of the fight, Jefferson thought, and in due time France and England might be slowed in their own destructive career by their need for American wheat and corn and cotton.

It was a man of reason's answer to a threatening situation, but reasonable answers are not always the most pleasing to people in general. American business was hurt by this Embargo Act. Merchants and bankers and traders everywhere screamed and shouted at Jefferson as their profits vanished and their stores closed, and their ships stood empty at the docks.

But Jefferson held to his course. Meantime, he was hurrying to make America more prepared, ordering fleets of gunboats and investigating the merits of submarines.

His inventiveness was stirred to action again. Even a peaceful nation should not allow itself to be so unprepared. Even a peaceful nation should have some sort of war fleet, ready for action in case of emergency. As for the ships being built so hastily, what would become of them when the threat had ended?

He remembered how, when he was in Italy, he had seen a system of dry docks in which ships could be kept in a partially finished state for years, ready for swift completion and launching. If the United States had a similar system of dry docks, the ships now being built could be stored safely through the years as insurance against future troubles.

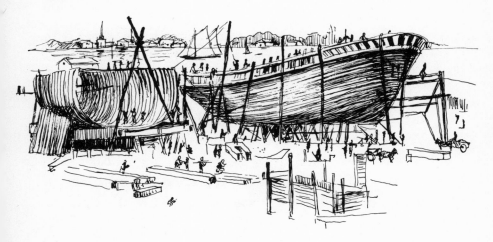

He got out his notes on the dry docks in Venice. He studied them and pondered how such dry docks might be revised and adapted for American needs.

At last he designed and had built a model of a dry dock which he was sure could easily be erected in the Navy Yard in Washington. The docks in Italy had been kept dry by constant pumping, but Jefferson had contrived to combine a lock with a common wet dock to achieve the same result without such labor. In a dock like this, and in similar docks elsewhere, Jefferson pro-

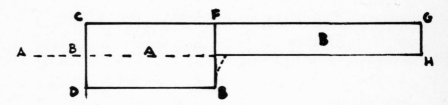

Jefferson's plan for a dry dock

posed to have "a proper number of vessels always ready to be launched."

He set up his model in the White House, along with the antlers, the bones and the war bonnets, and he invited the members of Congress to come and inspect it.

A special committee was set up to investigate the invention, and reported favorably. But the rest of the Congressmen were not so impressed. They sniffed and sneered and called it "visionary and impractical."

So Jefferson's dry dock remained a model, one of his inventions he never was able to put to the test.

Still, unpopular as his methods of dealing with the threat of war had been, his Embargo Act did have the result he wished. The United States did not go to war with England during the time he was President.

In 1809, his second term ended. He began packing up his fossils, his trophies of the West, his books, his music, his pounds and pounds of notes on the Indian language, his piles of notes on every other subject that interested him. Soon they were all on their way to Monticello.

It was a stroke of bad luck that caused the disappearance of all the notes on the Indian language during this trip. Some curious and greedy freight handler, intrigued by the weight of the trunk that held them, decided to make away with that particular part of the shipment.

Jefferson heard about the loss after he himself was back at Monticello. He was grieved, of course, and he thought of beginning again on the project some time. But he could not be cast down about anything for long. He was home again at last, on his hilltop, ready to retire from public life for good, to enjoy the serene and peaceful life of a farmer.

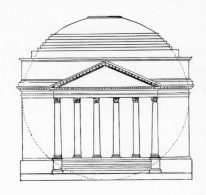

FOUNDER OF A LIBRARY, FOUNDER OF A UNIVERSITY, AND AN ARCHITECT AGAIN

I.

HE HAD DEVISED A WONDERFULLY LOGICAL COINAGE SYSTEM for his country. But for himself, in spite of meticulous records of all his expenses, he could not devise a way to keep out of financial difficulties.

There were good reasons, of course. In his years of public service he had been forced to spend much more than he was paid, often much more than the income from his farm could possibly justify. But it was also true that he was sometimes extravagant—where books and art were concerned. And he found it hard to resist buying lavish gifts for those he loved.

Now, in the years after he left Washington, things went from bad to worse financially, until suddenly it seemed he was on the brink of ruin.

It was all very unnerving. He had plunged into farming with the same zeal as always, and actually, the crops had never done better.

But the Napoleonic wars in Europe were having their effect on him as a farmer now. His wheat and tobacco were piling up, impossible to sell.

And there were still other reasons for his financial trouble. He had retired from public life, but the public had not given him up by any means. Thousands and thousands of Americans had always loved him. Now even those who had scoffed at him as "Mr. Mammoth," and the keeper of a bear garden, began to see him differently and think of him as figure of great wisdom. And all of them, it seemed, wanted to visit him at Monticello.

They came whether they had ever met him or not. They came with letters of introduction, or they came merely because some journey had brought them within fifty or a hundred miles of him and naturally that meant they were obliged to "drop in" for a visit.

It was impossible for Jefferson to turn anyone away.

Hospitality to a guest was bred in his bones, a way of life his father had charted for him years ago. Visitors, whoever they might be, had to be welcomed. They had to be fed. Very often they had to be lodged, and their horses and servants and families as well.

There were nights when Martha Randolph, her father's housekeeper these days, as well as the mother of a big family, was racking her brain to find sleeping places for fifty guests. Some guests came for a day and stayed a week. Some came for a week and stayed months.

Naturally, the expense involved in being host to a multitude was helping to drive him farther into debt. But Jefferson never thought of trying to limit his hospitality.

Instead, he sat in his library and pondered a question that has occupied a good many people from time to time across the centuries.

Where was he going to get money to pay his debts?

It may have been a very usual sort of question. But Jefferson, being who he was, came up with a very unusual answer.

He looked around at his books, literally thousands of them, collected over a course of fifty years. There were books on history and physics, astronomy, mathematics, religion—oh, think of a subject on which a book might have been written and Jefferson had a book on it.

He knew the value of his library and had long since decided that when he died, it should be offered to Congress to buy for the nation at whatever price Congress wanted to set.

Now he thought of the fact that in the recent war of 1812, which his successor, James Madison, had been unable to avoid, the British had done some grievous damage in Washington. Not only had they burned the Capitol and Executive Mansion, they had also burned the library of books which Congress had begun to collect.

Jefferson decided to offer his library to the nation immediately if Congress wished to purchase it. "Eighteen or twenty wagons," he wrote, "would place it in Washington in a single trip of a fortnight."

Congress did not hesitate when this rich offer was received, but accepted at once and offered $25,000 for the books.

$25,000! Jefferson breathed a sigh of relief, and paid off $15,000 worth of debts. And immediately began buying books again.

So he rescued himself from bankruptcy, and at the same time gave his country a fabulous collection of books which became the nucleus for today's world-famous Library of Congress.

II.

UNIQUE ANSWERS TO EVERYDAY QUESTIONS. JEFFERSON HAD been evolving responses like that since he was a boy.

Now, in his later years, there was still one great question he wanted to see answered in a practical, working fashion.

How could the citizens of a democracy be protected against gradually losing the precious rights which had been won for them at such a cost?

He had been sure of the answer for years. Long, long ago, he had begun working for free public education in Virginia.

"Whereas experience hath shewn that . . . those entrusted with power have, in time, and by slow operation, perverted it into tyranny . . . it is believed that the most effectual means of preventing this would be to illuminate . . . the minds of the people at large."

Basic elementary schools for all. After that, progressively advanced schools for the students whose capacities merited it, culminating in a university. That had been Jefferson's vision from the beginning, but the whole of the vision had never become a reality.

Briefly free from money worries, he began to turn his mind to this dream again. In particular, he began to think about the ideal university he dreamed of for Virginia. He thought of the courses such a school should offer. There should be much science, much more than most colleges were offering. There should be a course in agriculture, a subject not enough respected. Above all, and this was the part that was really revolutionary, this ideal university should be financed and supported by the state. Churches had been the sole support of institutions of higher learning long enough, Jefferson felt. He dreamed of a school free of all religious bias, free to instruct young minds in every worthwhile subject.

How? How was he to overcome the hostility of the churches to such a project? How was he to convince the legislators in Richmond of its importance?

It was not that he did not have enough else to think about these days.

His farming projects were going full-tilt. He was as busy as ever, experimenting with all sorts of fruits and plants. In his gardens and nurseries, he was raising rice and pecans and walnuts, figs from France, vetch from England, strawberries and corn from Italy, silk trees, apricots and a dozen other exotic plants and shrubs. He was also raising and observing many plants that Lewis and Clark had brought back from the West.

127

He was intrigued these days, too, with sheep raising, especially in experimenting with the Spanish Merino
breed. It seemed that the wool of this kind of sheep was
much finer than that of any breed currently being raised.
So Jefferson had some merino rams imported for his farm.

Delighted by his observations of them, he at once
began to plan a way in which every sheep raiser in Virginia could raise merinos. He himself would raise enough
sheep so that he could give a full-blooded ram to every
county in the state, a ram which would then be available
for breeding purposes to every farmer in that county.

His inventions were occupying a good deal of his
time. Along about now he had the moldboard for his
plow cast in iron, as thin as possible. He noted in his
Farm Book that it dug a furrow "9 inches wide and 6
inches deep with only two small horses or mules" to
draw it. And he added, with satisfaction, that it did
beautiful work.

Other inventions occurred to him. He had changed
some of his thinking since the days when he hoped
America would remain a primarily agricultural country.
The consequences of his own Embargo Act had shown
him that America needed to be able to manufacture all
sorts of goods for herself.

Beginning at home, he experimented with various
machines that would manufacture needed goods on a
small scale. He had spinning machines set up to manufacture the linen, cotton and wool needed to clothe his

Gardens at Monticello

family and servants, and he kept careful notes on their efficiency.

He experimented with growing his own flax, but found that crop unproductive. Hemp, however, grew well, but there was a problem in breaking it and beating it. So he invented a hemp-breaking machine which could easily be attached to the threshing machine. This invention, like the moldboard, he wanted to make available to everyone, so he decided to write up a description of it and have it published anonymously in various public papers.

No, he was not idle. There was all of this activity, and, of course, there were the guests, streaming in and out, all day and every day.

And there was the mail. Jefferson had always been a tireless letter writer. Now even he grew a little weary under his tremendous load of correspondence. People wrote to him from everywhere—old friends, mere acquaintances, utter strangers. And just as every guest had to be welcomed, every letter had to be answered, even if an average year brought him more than a thousand.

He was very glad these days to have the help of another man's invention to lighten the burden of this letter-writing somewhat. This was the polygraph, a writing desk with from two to five pens suspended from a mechanism above it in such a way that any movement made by one pen was exactly duplicated by the others.

Jefferson first acquired one of these ingenious writ-

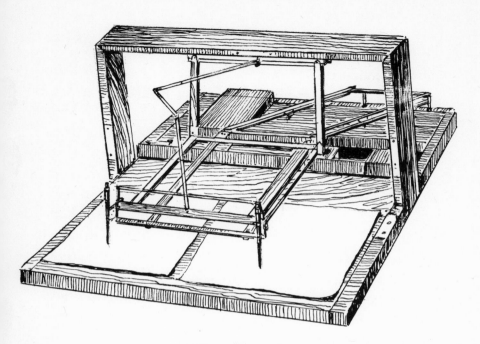

The polygraph

ing machines while he was President. He was so delighted with it that he not only used it constantly, he did his best to promote its general use everywhere. With its help he could write an original letter and have a duplicate for his files, or in cases where a form letter would serve, he could write several at once with ease. Sometimes, to show his friends how very well it worked, he would send them the duplicate of the letter he had written and keep the original himself.

And, of course, Jefferson thought of improvements for the polygraph: a better way of suspending the pens, a more compact case for the machine. He passed his suggestions on to the inventor who incorporated them

131

in later models.

Plainly, he was not sitting about in idleness in his retirement.

Still, the dream of the ideal university pursued him.

III.

HOW DOES A PERSON GO ABOUT FOUNDING A UNIVERSITY? How, in particular, could Jefferson achieve it, in those days when many churchmen viewed a project like his with indignation, and the legislators preferred not to think about it at all?

Through the years Jefferson had tried various methods. At one point he had hoped his own old school, William and Mary College, might be turned into a nonsectarian, state-supported institution. The church had squashed that. Other schemes he had pondered also came to nothing.

Now, in 1814, a better plan began evolving. It had two parts. One part involved a small academy which the state legislature had approved for Albemarle county. The other part involved a devoted friend of Jefferson's who was in the state legislature, and who was tirelessly ready to submit and resubmit whatever bills Jefferson wanted to further his educational dreams.

One way and another, Jefferson interested various

friends in the little Albemarle Academy. One friend was the former President, James Madison; one was the current President, James Monroe. The little academy was reorganized as a college—Central College—and contributions were sought to buy land and start building.

Jefferson contributed a thousand dollars to the fund, and when enough money had been collected, he chose and bought the land for the college site—two hundred high, beautiful acres just outside Charlottesville. It was no accident at all that these acres were visible from the terrace at Monticello, plain to see in every detail when viewed through the telescope that was mounted on the terrace.

Then, the site chosen, Thomas Jefferson, Architect, brought out some designs for a college on which he had

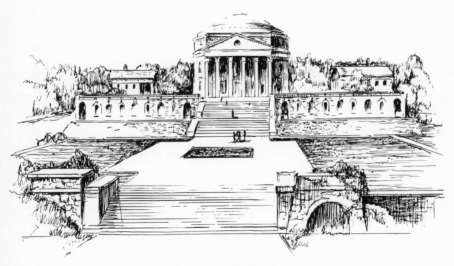

University of Virginia

been working, off and on, for several years.

Meantime, while all this was going on, his friend in the legislature had been proposing bill after bill, tailored by Jefferson, asking appropriations for free public schools, asking particularly an appropriation for a state university. Finally, the constant repetition of the bills had its effect. Public sentiment began to swing in favor of a state-supported school.

Gradually, gradually, the two parts of the plan began to mesh. Jefferson himself had staked out the site on the hill where the new college would be built. President Monroe had laid the cornerstone. The building was under way.

And then, at last, the legislature voted $15,000 to establish a state university.

It was not total victory—yet. The legislators had also appointed a commission to choose the site for the new school. Now Jefferson had to convince the men on the commission that the site on which his little Central College was already being built was just the site they wanted.

Once again, as so often before, he armed himself with an arsenal of facts and figures, and went forth to meet the commission. Men from all over Virginia were waiting for him, each of them ready to argue that the school should be built in his own particular region.

But Jefferson had his facts and his proofs. He had figures to prove that Charlottesville was one of the healthiest spots in the state. (Where else were there so many octogenarians?) He had a cardboard cut-out map of Virginia and spun it on a pencil point to prove that Charlottesville was in the center of the state geographically. He had a chart of the population of the state, by counties, to prove that Charlottesville was centrally located as to population also.

Then, as a final inducement, he mentioned the little college already under construction. It could be the basis for the new university if Charlottesville were chosen.

The commission was overwhelmed. No one could resist such an onslaught. Charlottesville was chosen as the site. The new little college would become the University of Virginia. Jefferson himself was chosen to supervise every aspect of establishing the new school.

It still was not the end of his struggle with the state legislature. Fifteen thousand dollars was nowhere near enough money to build and staff a university. Through the coming years, Jefferson would be constantly pressing for more funds, this friend and that friend carrying the bill into battle.

But the main victory was won. The state university was established, and just where he wanted it—so close to Monticello that he could keep a constant, watchful eye on every detail.

Now, as the buildings began to take shape, all the hours of thought and effort at his drafting board seemed more than justified.

135

Drafting desk

It was a very special group of buildings that Jefferson had designed for his university. To make it everything he dreamed of, he had called on all he had learned about architecture through the years. There was all the experience he had gained from designing and building and rebuilding Monticello. There was the State Capitol at Richmond he had designed. There were, as a matter of fact, half a dozen other buildings, private homes scattered through the Virginia hills, which he had also designed and helped build. One of them was his own second home, Poplar Forest, where he took refuge when guests overwhelmed him at Monticello.

What had he taken from all those buildings for this new and most important project?

136

First of all, there was the central building, domed and porticoed. This had always been his favorite architectural theme, based on the designs of Palladio he had first seen and loved so long ago. This gracious, classic building would be the focus of his plan.

But this was a university he was building, "an academical village" where young men would be coming to study and learn.

"It is the duty of those responsible for public buildings," he wrote to James Madison, "that they be designed

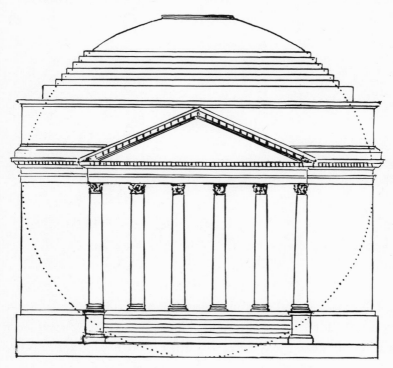

Jefferson's drawing for University of Virginia

as models for study and imitation."

So he had evolved a unique plan for the other buildings of his university. Each was to be a small replica of some architectural masterpiece—the theater of Marcellus, the Temple of Fortuna Virilis, and so on—each one an object lesson in art history.

Once again, Jefferson was looking at a problem as though it were brand-new, making the very buildings of his university part of the courses of instruction.

But with such a diversity of architectural styles, how could he achieve the beauty and harmony which were just as vital to him as utility?

His answer was again unique.

The domed, central building faced an open rectangle. On the two long sides of the rectangle were ranged the series of pavilions, each in a different style, each two stories high. (On the first floor of each would be the lecture room; above it, several rooms for the professor.) Between each of these pavilions were one-story dormitory rooms for the students. Each row of pavilions and dormitories was connected and unified by a one-story colonnade. The colonnade achieved what Jefferson was after, a harmony that encompassed all the different styles and tied them together into a beautiful whole.

This problem of harmony was not the only problem he had solved at his drafting board. He knew, for instance, that there is a trick of perspective to watch out for in planning anything like those two facing rows of

138

Colonnades at University of Virginia

pavilions. Unless proper compensation was made for it, half the effectiveness of those two colonnaded rows would be lost in distance perspective.

Jefferson, who had studied how the Greeks gently curved the eaves of their temples to achieve the *look* of a straight line, calculated to the inch the proper setback for each pavilion so as to maintain the look of an even row.

It was 1818, when the legislature finally made its appropriation and Jefferson could start building his university in earnest. He was seventy-five years old, no longer a young man. But he took on every detail with gusto and enthusiasm.

He himself was contractor and estimator, calculating the amount of stone, brick and timber needed, calculating the costs of the different types of material, seeking out the best and most efficient kind of stone, brick or timber for each particular use.

He hoped to use nothing but native materials for the whole school. Unfortunately, he found after months

139

of experimenting, and an outlay of $1,390, that Virginia's mica schist was not suitable for delicate ornamental detail so he had to write to Italy for carrara marble. But native timber and native stone made up the main body of the construction and the roofs of the pavilions and dormitories were covered with local slate.

He was eager to supervise every detail of the building. Every day he arose at dawn, as he had always done, soaked his feet in cold water (to prevent colds), spent an hour or so at his desk writing letters, spent some more time supervising the work on the farm or in the shops

140

at Monticello. Then, every working day, he mounted his good horse, Eagle, and rode the four miles down the mountain to Charlottesville, to watch and help with whatever part of the construction was under way.

There was a shortage of trained workmen. Often he found himself teaching some slow countryman how to lay bricks, or how to mortice a joint.

He wrote to Europe for stone-carvers because there were no craftsmen in the United States skilled enough to carve the graceful pillars or the enriched designs of fruit and flowers he had planned for the pediments and eaves. But even with such practiced workers on hand, he kept his eye on every bit of work. A visitor who found him at the university site one day saw him take a chisel from an Italian sculptor to show him personally exactly how to turn a volute on a pillar.

So the weeks and months and finally the years went by, with the dream slowly taking shape. Neighbors grew used to the sight of the tall, erect old man, riding his horse down the mountain in the morning, back up again at night. Bundled onto his saddle, he carried another invention of his which was useful these days—a collapsible seat, contrived of three legs which could be opened out to support a stretched piece of cloth. Now and then Jefferson sat down on it, but there was always something to call him to his feet again.

There were some days, not many, when for one reason or another he could not make the trip down the

141

mountain. That was when the telescope on the terrace came in handy. If anything seemed to be going amiss, Jefferson quickly wrote a note about it and despatched that down the mountain. The hired overseer knew there was no use in trying to escape the eye of that one, up on the hill.

And, of course, the actual building was not all that engaged Jefferson's attentions. He was responsible also for acquiring the staff who would teach in the university when it was finished.

So, along with all his other correspondence, he was writing to friends here and abroad for their recommendations on the most learned, talented professors in the various subjects he had planned for the university's curriculum. He was reviewing, in his own mind, all the men whose writings or whose teachings had impressed him. He was writing to England, to France, to Scotland, to the professors he had finally selected as the very best available.

At last, in 1825, almost eleven years after he had first begun work on his dream, the University of Virginia was ready to open its doors.

March 7, 1825, was the great day. All the professors had arrived from Europe. Trustees of the school, neighbors, townspeople, friends from all over who had done their part in achieving the dream, made their way up the hill to the lovely central building.

Still tall and erect for all his eighty-two years,

Central building, University of Virginia

Jefferson greeted them. His manner was as quiet and gracious as ever, his voice as mild, but his heart was full of pride and triumph.

"And ye shall know the truth and the truth shall make you free." That was the motto he had chosen for the University. And at last the University was ready, proud and beautiful on its hill. Within it were the men who were equipped to teach what they knew of the

143

truth, about science and philosophy and history, so that more and more young people could not only know what it was to be free, but how to guard and cherish that freedom as long as they lived.

. . . AND MORE

WHAT IS A PLOW?

A plow is a tool designed to break the hard crust of the earth and make it ready for new seed.

All his life, Jefferson had been plowing, breaking up the hard crust of tradition and prejudice, loosening up people's minds so they would be ready for new ideas, new ideals.

All his life he had been planting, too, the new ideas that he had garnered from everywhere—from reading his thousands of books, from asking questions of thousands of people, from observing with interest and curi-

145

osity every single thing that passed before his eyes.

For he saw everything as though it were brand-new, and asked himself questions about it. How does it work? Could it work better? Is it useful? Is it good? Is is beautiful?

Because he was so willing to question everything, there had always been those people who thought he was a Godless man. To them, a true believer was someone who accepted everything as it was; pain, fear and the tyranny of kings along with everything else. Unhappy those things might be, but since they had always existed, they were part of God's plan.

But "rebellion to tyrants is obedience to God," Thomas Jefferson said. And rebellion to everything that held men's minds in ignorance and fear was obedience to God as well, for "Almighty God created man's mind free."

So he had his own kind of religion, and if it was not one that was easily understood by men who were more interested in dogma than in deeds, it was one that sustained him and inspired him all his life long.

The God he "acknowledged and adored" was "the creator and benevolent governor of the world." Jefferson looked forward to the day when men's minds would be strengthened by education to accept "the genuine and simple religion of Jesus" unmuffled by any mystery.

His own interest in the simple religion of Jesus had led him during the days when he was President to com-

146

pile a "Life of Jesus." He took the four Gospels and cut out every sentence and every word that was not an exact report of Jesus' own words. He arranged what was left in chronological order and according to subject matter, regardless of how the quotations had been arranged in the Gospels.

"A more beautiful or precious morsel of ethics I have never seen," he told a friend. "It is a document in proof that I am a *real Christian*."

Now, when he was an old man at Monticello, there were those who wished that the "Life of Jesus" he had compiled might be published. He had also written a concise summary of his beliefs to a friend, and that friend asked if he could make it public.

"No, my dear sir, not for the world," Jefferson wrote back. "Into what a nest of hornets would it thrust my head."

Warring sectarians, blinded by their own beliefs, would never accept anything so simple as Jefferson's credo, based on Jesus' own words, "That to love God with all thy heart, and thy neighbor as thyself, is the sum of religion."

So Jefferson's little book on Jesus was never published in his lifetime.

It did not really matter. His life had been one long example of what he believed, and if it was not so clear to everyone then as it has grown through the years, it is plain now that he had always been obedient to the

147

Monticello, with dome added

God who created man's mind free.

Free his mind had been when he was young. It was still free and active when he was old. He was eighty-three and knew he would not live much longer. Now and then he could take short rides on horseback. Now and then he could take pleasure in entertaining at dinner the professors and students from his beloved University down the hill.

But the Thomas Jefferson who had always been designing and sketching out plans was sketching a design for his own monument now.

And the Thomas Jefferson who had always liked to summarize facts, weigh them, and ponder their relative meaning, was summarizing his own life.

He thought of all he had done and all he might say he had accomplished. He had been Vice-President, and Secretary of State, and President of the United States. He had been the founder of a great political party and he had bought the Louisiana Territory for the United States. His advice and his counsels were embodied in crucial documents from the Constitution to the Monroe Doctrine. He had built beautiful buildings, invented useful things and written useful books.

From all these achievements and many more, he singled out just three to inscribe on his tombstone. He wanted to be remembered as the author of the Declaration of Independence, which he had written back in 1776; as the author of the Statute for Religious Freedom

150

in Virginia, which he had proposed and fought for in 1779; and finally, he wanted to be remembered as the Father of the University of Virginia, a dream he had achieved in his old age.

He chose three, all focused on freedom. We can remember more. We can read book after book, all relating different achievements during the course of his long and incredibly active life.

And we can remember the plow. This, too, helps make men free.

CHRONOLOGY

Born: Shadwell, Albemarle
    County, Virginia   April 13, 1743

Student at William and Mary
    College   1760 - 1762

Law student at Williamsburg   1762 - 1767

Lawyer   1767 - 1774

Representative, House of
    Burgesses, Virginia   1769 - 1776

Married   1772

Delegate to Second Continen-
    tal Congress   1775 (May - August)

Delegate to Second Session of
    Second Continental
    Congress   1776 (May - September)

Member of Virginia House of
    Delegates   1776 - 1779

Governor of Virginia   1779 - 1781

Death of his wife   1782

Delegate to Congress from
    Virginia   1783 - 1784

Minister Plenipotentiary, then Ambassador to France	1784 - 1789
Secretary of State of the United States	1790 - 1793
Farmer	1794 - 1797
Vice-President of the United States	1797 - 1801
President of the United States	1801 - 1809
Sage of Monticello	1809 - 1826
Died at Monticello	July 4, 1826

A SELECTED BIBLIOGRAPHY

Berman, Eleanor Davidson. *Thomas Jefferson Among the Arts.* New York Philosophical Library, 1947.

Criss, Mildred. *Jefferson's Daughter.* New York: Dodd, Mead & Company, 1948.

Curtis, William Eleroy. *The True Thomas Jefferson.* Boston: J. B. Lippincott, 1901.

Frary, I. T. *Thomas Jefferson, Architect and Builder.* Richmond, Virginia: Garrett & Massie, Inc., 1931.

Jefferson, Thomas. *The Autobiography of Thomas Jefferson.* New York and London: G. P. Putnam, 1914.

———. *Collected Papers of Thomas Jefferson.* Princeton: Princeton University Press, 1950–.

———. *Thomas Jefferson's Farm Book.* Princeton: Princeton University Press, 1953.

———. *Thomas Jefferson's Garden Book.* Philadelphia: The American Philosophical Society, 1944.

Kimball, Sidney Fiske. "Thomas Jefferson as an Architect." *Architectural Quarterly* of Harvard University, 1914.

Lambeth, William A. and Manning, W. H. *Thomas Jefferson as an Architect and Designer of Landscapes.* Boston: Houghton Mifflin Co., 1913.

Malone, Dumas. *Jefferson and His Time*. Boston: Little, Brown & Co., 1948.

Martin, Edwin T. *Thomas Jefferson: Scientist*. Henry Schuman, 1952.

Mayo, Bernard. *Jefferson Himself: The Personal Narrative of a Many-Sided American*. Boston: Houghton Mifflin Co., 1942.

Moscow, Henry and editors of American Heritage. *Thomas Jefferson and His World*. New York: American Heritage Publishing Company-Golden Press, 1960.

Padover, Saul K. *Jefferson: A Great American's Life and Ideas*. New York: Harcourt Brace, 1942. New American Library, 1952.

———., editor. *A Jefferson Profile, As Revealed in His Letters*. New York: The John Day Company, 1956.

Parrington, Vernon L. *The Colonial Mind*. New York: Harcourt Brace, 1927, 1954.

Patton, John Shelton. *Monticello and Its Master*. Charlottesville: The Michie Co., 1928.

Rhodes, Thomas L. *The Story of Monticello*. Washington, D.C.: American Publishing Co., 1928.

Wilstach, Paul. *Jefferson and Monticello*. New York: Doubleday, Page & Co., 1925.

INDEX

INDEX

159

THE AUTHOR

In THOMAS JEFFERSON, HIS MANY TALENTS, Johanna Johnston again pursues her interest in bringing to life great figures of the past whose very greatness has made them seem somehow remote and unreal.

The author of THE STORY OF HANNIBAL, in which a long-ago general again becomes young and brave and eager, and JOAN OF ARC, the story of a young girl all alone on a well-nigh impossible mission, Miss Johnston has also written many books for younger children as well, among them the imaginative CLOSE YOUR EYES and SUGARPLUM with its tiny doll character. For several years she wrote for radio, both free-lance and as a member of the Columbia Broadcasting System, specializing in programs for children. One of her favorites was the popular "Let's Pretend" fairy-tale theater.

Miss Johnston lives in New York City and has a daughter, Abby, who is rapidly becoming as interested as her mother in creating books for young people.

THE ARTIST

Paintings by Richard Bergere have been exhibited in museums in Chicago, New York City, Philadelphia, and Dayton, Ohio. Versatile as well as creative, and holding degrees in both art and architecture, he does mural painting and advertising work in addition to book illustrations, and has also taught art and interior design.

Mr. Bergere's own book about architecture, FROM STONES TO SKYSCRAPERS, for which his wife Thea wrote the text, has received wide acclaim and contains over 100 exquisite drawings in black and white.

The Bergeres reside on Long Island with their small daughter.